THE
AGONY
THE
EBONY

THE AGONY THE EBONY

SARITA CARDWELL

The Agony The Ebony

Copyright © 2019 by Sarita Cardwell. All rights reserved.

No part of this publication may be reproduced, stored in a retrieval system or transmitted in any way by any means, electronic, mechanical, photocopy, recording or otherwise without the prior permission of the author except as provided by USA copyright law.

The opinions expressed by the author are not necessarily those of URLink Print and Media.

1603 Capitol Ave., Suite 310 Cheyenne, Wyoming USA 82001
1-888-980-6523 | admin@urlinkpublishing.com

URLink Print and Media is committed to excellence in the publishing industry.

Book design copyright © 2019 by URLink Print and Media. All rights reserved.

Published in the United States of America

ISBN 978-1-64367-698-2 (Paperback)
ISBN 978-1-64367-697-5 (Digital)

17.07.19

Contents

The Pact 9
The Throwback 12
The Legend 15
Super 19
Orphy Dorphy 24
In Africa 28
Hungry Thieves 33
Hip Hop Hustle 38
Common Killer 43
Change 46
Amozeke Receiving 49
Amozeke! Amazon! Amozula! 57
Lawnmower Noise 66
Two 69
Saint Turned Skeezer 72
Way up North! 74
Rowing Machine 78
Real 81
Live Love 83
Hungry Thieves II 85
Horse 90
Feet Brand New 92
Dreamboat 93
Wisdom 95
Ugly Cats 97
Trail Blazers 99
The Baroness Lizzy 101
Strutting My Stuff 104
The Dream 106

Samoseam	108
The Creed	110
Pipe Dreams	112
Person	115
The Word	117
One Ace	120
Man Hands	122
Make You Wish That You Was	126
Old Man River	128
The Tree	131
Mt. Kilimanjaro	133
Lizzy's Boredom II	134
Listen!	136
Kinks	138
The Deed	141
Let Us Be	143
Afrane Luminous	145
Amozeke! Amazon! Amo-Africans!	146
Ain't Misbehaving	152
Africa	155
The Power	156
Dream, Dream, Freedom's Bell	158
Dream	159
Earl	161
Facing The Honest Truth Like Ruth	162
Long Gone	164
I Must Lead	167
Have-Not Less-Got	169
Hope	171
Hungry Thieves III	172
I Live In A World	174
For a Little Heaven on Earth Drug	175
Bright Eyes	178
Ashy	179
A Girl Called Stupid	180
The Talk	182
Wider Than The River	183

Dreams And Desires	185
The Escapade	186
For Real	189
Hate	191
Spread Love	194
Perfect World	197
Greatness Found	200
The Blood	203
Perfect Fit	205
Open Road	207
Rat Race	208
Piglatin	211
Educated	213
The Winning Hand	215
The Virgins	216
Riper-Viper Pastures	217
Been Born	218
Higher Plane	219
Your Mind	221
The Young	223
Snakes and the Legend	225
The Lovers	227
Wanted	228
Better Days	230
The Joy	233
A Finer Line	234
A Finer Line Part 2	236
Give It A Rest	237
Downhill	239
The Rarest Folk	242
The Answer	244
The High and the Mighty	246
The Ends the Means	247
The Good Song	249
Meet and Greet	251
It's Clear	254
Somebody's Sweet Fool	257

The Pact

I was born in wealth
grew up in shame
folks around the way
remembered my name...
Born near the falls
Blessed to walk the
hallowed halls...

Born, born,
I made a pact-
Born, born,
devil get back!

I was born in wealth
grew up in shame
starvation had my
number
poverty knew my name!
Swore to the very end
As many hearts broken
I would mend!

Born, born,
betcha bite a chip...
Born, Born,
Child give me no lip!

I was born, raised...
went to school...
I was praised...
When other folks wasn't...
I had a good name
Whether it gets done or doesn't-
-Worked hard through
the pain...

But I made the grade...
Wish I could get paid...
Silence was golden...
Pressure was the pain!

Born, born,
I made a pact...
Born, born,
devil get back!

I was born in wealth,
grew up in shame...
starvation had my number,
and poverty knew my name!
I had a good name...
went from trouble to
fame...

Fame and fortune,
Fortune and fame...
Which comes first
the baby or the name?
The name game
The same rain
Washing over my head...
So cold, I felt like
I was dead!

The same old system
Bless 'em, confess 'em
Miss 'em, and diss 'em!

Born, born,
I made a pact...
Born, born,
devil get back!

Which would you
hold on to?
Which would you
throw away?
Taking it all for
granted....
Wishing that you
could only stay...

Born, born,
I made a pact...
Born, born,
devil get back!

The Throwback

It could be one of those
good things that keep
you warm

But afraid that if I
blink I miss it,
and it be gone!

Come back, throw back,
That mellow curve...
Come back, Lo-jack,
So much action
To singe the raw nerve!

And hands of steel
Hands of feeling
Deep down in your heart
And you know he's for- realing
Without knowing where to start,

COME BACK-
THROW BACK- that mellow curve...

COME BACK-
TO LO-JACK
AND GET READY FOR THE WORLD!

Mellow curve,
Mellow curve...
All the JOY WATISSIMO'S
IN THE WORLD!

Sing you a song...
String you along....
Sing it when I'm long-Gone!
Throwback that mellow curve
With a brassy, sassy, song!

Hear me now and
hear me well...
Life's sweet golden moments
Are the sounds of freedom bells

Ring-Ring,
Sing-sing,
Sing wrong,
Ring wrong!

Go back,
Throw back,
Come back
To LO-Jack!

GO back
Throw back
Come back
TO LO-JACK!

Throwback, go back in time...
Go back, to the place that
started the rhyme!

Go back to the place that
started the blues...
There's just going to be a problem
IF YOU SNOOZE!
Use the time wisely
Live a little, learn a little,
Because life's full of Surprises!

Give a little... Live a little...
One step at a time...

En Amour Amozeke you, to keep you,
   so that you can Amo-Arrive!

The Legend

There once was a girl
named Dee...And if you
laughed your crooked
laugh, and showed
your crooked smile...
She begun to walk a
country ole' mile.
laughing as she went
out the door (where
she always stood)...
each person would
watch her laugh her-
self a country ole' mile!
which to her was good...

with her good friend no-
name (who remains a
mystery)
Like an apple a day
keeps the doctor away...

here's the good one
that got away... walk
with me three miles
a day...And we'll see

you at the party,
Or legend club...
That's just like your
average house or pub!

It's extraordinary
With her all-knowing
look
Said: You're talking
too much death, you
old crook!

The legend never dies
The legend down-to-earth!
Because the legend
never dies...take some
chances for what it's
worth!

If you talks a crooked
talk...and you walks a
crooked walk...and you
smiles a crooked smile...
Walk to the legendary
legends club...where it's
just like your average
house or pub.

And all you heard was
laughter...you couldn't
run or go faster! You had
to stay and outsmart the
master of all masters...
If you can't catch up-just
run faster!

Smoke flowed out of the
mouth and out of the
windows...smoke flowed
through the air...
This is why the legend won't
stop or die in months...
But don't let it catch your
hair!

Because if you has a
crooked laugh, smoke
comes out of your mouth...
You'd get on your horse and
clippedy-clop,
down a country old mile!

The laughter, the legend,
the label won't fade away
or die...
The laughter, the legend,
the label-and you smokes
your smokes and you smiles
your crooked smile...

Because the legend is rumored
to be a place of great evils...
Dee and her friend No-Name
were really great deceivers!
So much smoke that it travels
through the room... but don't
let it catch your hair...

So to ask your when's and
to ask your why's...the laughter,
the legend, the label never fades

away or dies...
So to ask you when's and why's...
I say the legend never closes
or dies...

Who wants to live the legend?
Who's gonna steal the show?
Who wants to live the legend-
because you think you're gonna
know!

The laughter, the legend, the
label
won't fade away or die...
Smoke goes through the room...
And you ran a good, country
ole' mile!

Because it travels through
the room and into the air...
It travels on and on, but don't
let it catch your hair!

Who wants to live the
legend? Who wants to let
it die?
Who wants to live the legend?
And you told your crooked lies!

Though into you, and beyond
the old mirror...
What lives on is what's out there...

Though into you, and beyond
the old mirror...
What lives on is what's out there!

Super

Superman, Super bitch!

What you gonna do?

I say what you gonna do

When those walls

All fall down on you?!

I say what you gonna do

When those walls all

Fall down on you!

Jump when they ask

How high ?

Or wait it out like

A prince in a high

Tower?

Is a bull - Or a bully,

Is a bully

To the bitch!

Is a bird?

Is a plane!

Is supper bitch!

Once treating for tricks

Got more tricks than sticks,

Super what you want,

Super is what you get!

On your plate or in

Your face!

Jupiter and Kansas

have met!

Is super what you want?

Supper is what you get!

On your plate,

Or in your face,

Gonna get on your case!!!

Just in time,

This is the place,

Or, should I throw it

in your face?

Hair styled and dressed

To match!

Beauty and the beast

Got love to catch!

Hair styled and dressed

to match...beauty and the

Beast got love to catch!

Beauty in the deep,

Beauty in the west-

Beauty and the beast

Got love to confess!

Confess it, confess it,

Confess it to wit...

Super is what you want

Supper is what you get!

I say what you gonna do

when it all falls on you?

Beast and the beauty,

Beauty and the beast,

This is what I'm saying:

Three to the East!

Super is what

You want- Supper is what

you get...

Beauty and the beast

got love to get!

Beauty and the beast

Beast and the beauty-

Stomping my feet...

Shaking my booty!

Sha--booty!

The Beauty!

Beast in the deep,

Beauty in the west...

Beauty and the beast

Got love to 'fess!

Orphy Dorphy

Orphy-Dorphy is what she's called,
She makes such a mess,
And then she's gone,
Just like a pest!

Orphy-Dorphy is what she's called,
Brain like a bubble,
Jezebels mirror image,
Or should I call her Jezze bubble?

Orphy-Dorphy is what she's called,
She sleeps in the nude,
You can't ever be too careful,
Her ass is just plain rude!

Orphy-Dorphy is what she's called,
And this I must confess:
She ain't nothin but trouble,
And just a snotty old pest!

Orphy-Dorphy is what she's called,
Boys trying to have something to see,
When they come to look at Orphy,
They come from as far as Riley street,

Orphy-Dorphy,
Orphy-Dorphy...

Lizzy-Kizzy-Boredom...

Orphy-Dorphy,
Orphy-Dorphy,

Leave and take
Some more of them...

Orphy-Dorphy,
Orphy-Dorphy,

Lizzy-Kizzy-Boredom...

Orphy-Dorphy,
Orphy-Dorphy,

Leave and take
Some more of them...

Orphy-Dorphy,
Orphy-Dorphy,

Brain like a bubble...

Orphy-Dorphy,
Orphy-Dorphy,

You're asken' for trouble...

Orphy-Dorphy,
Orphy-Dorphy,

Brain like a bubble...

Orphy-Dorphy,
Orphy-Dorphy,

You're asken' for trouble!

Orphy-Dorphy,
Orphy-Dorphy,

Start using your head...

Orphy-Dorphy,
Orphy-Dorphy,

You just been misled...

Jezebel-Jezzebubble,
Stop looking for trouble...

Jezebel-Jezzebubble...
I'm not your double!

Jezebel-Jezzebubble...
Just make a choice...

Jezebel-Jezzebubble...
Why can't you rejoice?

Search deep in your heart
And get you some pride...

Search deep in your heart...
Get a brand new start!

Orphy-Dorphy,
Orphy-Dorphy,

Lizzy-Kizzy-Boredom...

Orphy-Dorphy,
Orphy-Dorphy,

Leave and take some more of 'em...

Orphy-Dorphy,
Orphy-Dorphy,

Lizzy-Kizzy-Boredom...

Orphy-Dorphy,
Orphy-Dorphy,

Leave and take
Some more of 'em!

In Africa

In Africa-
Where the saga
begins-

the Amozekes
will detect
when the tides
will come in
Where all the
people had ruled,
and they all was kin!

It's often hard to
detect when the
tides do come in!

I wonder who?
Boy is it you?

Sweat in the sun…
-you don't have have fun!

A risk and a chance
to charm will
enhance our stories

of old that
are bold
tragics told!

A risk and a chance
to charm
will enhance
Our stories of old
that are bold tragics told!

In Africa where the
saga begins

the Amozekes will
detect where the
tides do begin

where all the people
had ruled

and they all was kin!

its often hard to accept
when the tides do begin!

Amozekes, Amazons all over the nation
Amozulas, Amo-Khans to strengthen
The nation!

The old, bold, stories told!
Tragics lost, treasures gained, stories of old
Amozekes, Amazons and legends
unfold!

Amozekes, Amazons, and
the story was told!

Come fly with me!
To our destiny!
And together
we'll see! what
conclusions will be!

In Africa...
Where the world begins...

The outer seas
will
collect
What the tides
do bring in...

From where the people
had ruled
And
They all was kin
It's often hard
To predict where the
tides do begin!

I wonder who?
boy is it you?

Sweat in the sun...
You don't have fun!

A risk and a chance
will serve to enhance

Our stories of old
That are bold tragics
told!

A risk and a chance
will sever to enhance
Our stories of old
That are bold
Tragics told!

In my lions den
There's trouble
and sin...
Don't beat the
drums so slow-
Beat them fast
Then I'll Know!

In my lions den
There's trouble
and sin...
Don't beat the
drums so slow-
Beat them fast!
Then I'll know!

So many people!
So many rulers!
Not many sorrows...

Don't break the rules

A risk and a chance
will serve to enhance
Our stories of old
That are bold tragics
Told!

A risk and a chance
will serve to enhance
Our stories of old
That are bold tragics
told!

Hungry Thieves

What's this I see...some faces
Pressed against my window pane?
Whose hungry thieves are those...
And why'd they come back again?

Because they get all hungry
For the grub I got...
They act like I'm the only
One in the world...
Should they get what I got?

I wish I could wish 'em up something....
Something they ain't got...
Something to make them go away,
So their stomachs can be in a knot!

In the winter It gets cold,
Have to shovel the snow...
Just where did these hungry thieves come from?
That...I just don't know...

But I work hard
For the grub I got...
But who the heck are these hungry thieves?
Because their mother...I just am not!

I could pull down my shade
But their shadows still show...
I could toss 'em a bread loaf
But they'd come back for more...

Their mouths say "open the door"
But I won't let them in...
Their minds say grab the grub
These thieves are committing a sin!

Who made these monsters?
Somehow...I'll make 'em go!
Who showed 'em my house?
Now that...I just don't know...

God forgive me if it's witchcraft
I'm willing to admit...
But if I can't stop it
I'd be willing to try and quit!

If they can't help it
I'll pray and ask God to guide their feet home...
And make this their last dance...
And just leave me alone!

Let their thieving thoughts crumble
Turn to ashes and dust...
Let them scatter in the wind...
And stop watching my house!

Let their thieving thoughts never rise
To eyeball my grub...
Turn their sunny skies gray....
My house ain't no pub!

Let them never to imagine...
How they can take my grub...
Let God drop 'em down a big bread loaf...
From the heavens above!

For they want my attention
To ask for my grub...
But their big old eyes just stare...
I wish for the heavens to take me above!

Because they want me to do a favor
For some old fools...
Will eat me out of house and home...
For they hate to follow rules!

Why should I sit hear...
Just so nice and quiet?
While they eat everything up...
And cause in my house a riot!

And then what next?
What else would start looking good?
But this whole house
I should pick it up and move!

But where could I go?
Except the place that Moses stood...
For they wouldn't cross desert...
Because they'd die of thirst before they moved!

If they were all sponges
They'd soak stuff up...
They'd soak up whatever grub I have
And take it out of my house!

They want to play around
So close to forever...
Then turn around and eat all day long...
No matter what the weather!

Where are the good folks,
Who earns their way,
But these thieves just wanna take,
And think they are earning their pay!

Why can't what I do in my house
Be just so quiet and private?
Because the grub I eat
Seems to keep the sky lit!

I wish the neighbor
Was the ice-cream man...
He would pick them all up...
And take them out of my hands!

And now I've had enough
To turn my head away...
I'm gonna fight fire with fire...
Or give them their way!

But what's this outside me window?
And what could it be?
Nothing short of a miracle
But the biggest apple tree!

So I stood their in awe
And went to see if I got
Not one basket, but two...
To carry them out!

And for all they stood there
For the grub I got...
When I find them two baskets
I'm gonna carry them out...

It took me a while
Searched high and low...
And there they was
Right behind my door!

I carried them outside
And climbed up the tree...
And I filled up them baskets...
Just for them to be happily watching me!

As they look up in wonder
I possess all the joy,
To invite these fools in,
To eat till they can't no more!

As they look up in wonder
From the top to the bottom of the tree...
Their eyes filled with joy
And they smiled at me!

And there I left them
To sit in the sun...
To eat till their hearts content
And boy, was they having fun!

And I know this for a fact...
This problem was just one...
That I never thought I'd solve..
Till I looked...and seen the sun!

Hip Hop Hustle

Hip hop hustle!

Glory to the muscle!

That made it all happen...

experiences just for rapping!

And you knew that

dancing was here to stay...

All work-no play-

Gonna make you change

your ways...!

Hip hop hustle

Glory to the muscle

That made it all happen...

fingers toes are tapping

And tapping to the beat

It was the beat of the streets!

And for the lessons

you learned along the way

Like no pain no gain,

And it makes you wanna say...

You got to see it!

To believe it!

You got to feel it!

And you got to start dreaming it!

See it...

Believe it!

Feel it...

Dream it!

Hip hop hustle

Glory to the muscle...

That made it all happen...

The music, the beats

Made for rapping!

To the music, to the beat,

Shake, shake, shake!

To the music, to the beat,

Shake it to the east...

Shake it to the west...

Shake it to the very

Ones that you love the best!

Hip hop hustle...

Glory to the muscle!

I say Hip Hop Hustle!

Glory to the muscle!

And you knew that

Music was here to stay -

Learn life's lessons...

Try to change your ways

change your ways...

    Here's how it stands:

    If it's music you must make..

    Then try to be positive and

    A strong rapping man!

    See it, believe it!

    Feel it, dream it!

    See it, believe it!

    Feel it, dream it!

    Hip Hop Hustle!

    Glory to the muscle!

    That made it all

    Happen...experiences

    For rapping...

    Snapping my fingers...

    Stomping my feet-

To the music

To the rhythm

To the rhythm

To the beat!

Snapping my fingers.....

Stomping my feet-

To the music

To the rhythm

To the rhythm

To the beat!

Common Killer

Common killer,
Common saint,
Common killer-

The devil's not a saint!

Common killer,
Common saint,
Is what you believe in...

The common saint!?

Good God!
Good gold!
Thank Nguensta!

Because here I
Come-stah!

I create the rhymes
So you can feel the
Rushes!

Get ready for the world,
you and me...

Get ready for the world,
it's my pearl, see?

I sing
I sang
I sung
though here I come,
it's the real place to be....

I sing
I sang
I sung!

I ain't crying!
I am trying! to be just me!

I ain't crying!
I am trying! to be
totally free!

If it's fish! I'll scamper out and
buy it...If it's fish! I will fry it!
Fry fish! Fry you! Surely,
you must have a clue!
As to
what I'm doing here...
My rhymes are here to
stay...
The dirty dozen plus one...
I'm slap-happy in my own
standing family way!

Common killer
Common saint
It's so hot...that I
just might faint!

To have this gift is great
The African land is good
We thank the Living God
For the knowledge is our food!

Paint me a beautiful river
-Started by a stream-
Paint me a beautiful river
though as impossible as
it may seem!

There is nothing impossible
unto you...
There is nothing impossible
for You! You! You!

Common killer...
Common saint...
Common killer...

That's why the devil's
just not a saint!

Change

Ever since the day we met,
Dawn of a new day arising,
The saying is still not so very strange,
Except I'm sitting here waiting for my man to change,

School days for the life of me,
School days for the twice of me,
Sitting here together we rearrange,
All the while sitting here waiting my man to change.

Bet on a dummy and loose all your money,
Fools always want to disarrange,
They want dollars for no common sense,

Wait your change
Don't rearrange…

Wait your change
Don't rearrange…

Nothing's far from the honest truth,
I'm facing it just like Ruth,
Nothing's far from the honest truth,
I'm standing here facing it
Just like Ruth…

Because I'll have gray hairs
And grow old till I was dead-
Waiting for you to come out your cheating ways...

Because you'll never find me
Waiting up for you
And God knows the day
When and If you change...

Quit trying to rearrange...
Or just change!

You say that what the world needs
Is love sweet love?

Wait your change,
Don't rearrange...

Wait your change,
Don't rearrange...

You say what the world needs
Is love sweet love?

Wait your change,
Don't rearrange...

Wait your change,
Don't rearrange...

Because when and if you call…
Don't try to rearrange!

Since it's outta sight outta mind,
You can wait your 'cotton-picking' change!

When and if you call…
Don't try to rearrange!

Since it's out of sight, out of mind,
You can wait your 'cotton-picking' change!!

Amozeke Receiving

IF:
The amozula way
is your way of life

Then:

The gift of being
is amozeke-receving...
Then keep amozeke-believing
and keep hope alive...
there is a reason for fate
if you amozeke-arrive!

You of the African race
Keep on amozeke-surviving
and keep up the pace!

amozeke-prove
before you amozeke-move!
Continue to survive, if you can
amozeke-arrive!

LET'S:

Come together as
a people...let's come together
as one tribe...

Count the miracles
Count the moments...
Do goodness and
amozeke-strive!

Count the blessings
and the good times
(of triumph and endeavor)

Count the blessings
and the good times...
and catch the amozeke- vibe!

We the African people
come together as one
tribe...
Catch the vibe,
Catch the feeling,
And amozeke-arrive!

We the African people
let's come together as
one tribe...

Catch the vibe,
Catch the feeling,
And amozeke-arrive!

IF

Your family is a tribe...
Going way back,
Going way back,
Going way back,
To when Nzingha was alive...

Catch the feeling,
Catch the vibe,
And amozeke-arrive!

THEN:

The gift of being
Is amozeke-receiving
There is a reason for fate
If you keep amozeke-believing!

You just gotta Nzingha-receive it!
You just gotta Nzingha-believe it!

You just gotta
amozeke- take-it
You just gotta
amozeke-make-it!

IF:

Your family is a tribe...
Going way back,
Going way back,
Going way back,
To when the great Shaka
was alive-

Then catch the feeling,
Catch the vibe,
Catch the feeling,
And amozeke-arrive!

The gift of being is
amozeke-receiving...
There is a reason for fate
if you keep amozeke-believing!

You just gotta Shaka-believe-it!
You just gotta Shaka-receive-it!

AND:

Catch the feeling,
Catch the vibe,
Catch the feeling,
And amozeke-arrive!

OR:

Catch the feeling,
You just gotta believe it!
Catch the feeling,
Straight hair is when
You receive it!

Catch the feeling,
Catch the vibe,
And amozeke-arrive!

IF:

the Amozula way
Is your way of life
Then the gift of being
Is amozeke-receiving
No stress or strife!

Keep amozeke-believing
And keep hope alive...
There is a reason for
Fate if you amozeke-arrive!

YOU:

Of the African race
Keep on amozeke-surviving
Seeing that you are
amozeke-arriving...

KEEP UP THE PACE!

amozeke-prove before
You amozeke-move!

Continue to strive
Even as you amozeke-arrive!

Let us come together
As a people...
Let us come together
As one tribe...

Count the miracles,
Count the moments,
Do goodness, and,
Amozeke strive!

Count the blessings,
Count the good times,
And catch the amozeke vibe!

We the African people,
Come together as one tribe

Catch the vibe,
Catch the feeling,
While it is amozeke-receiving!

We as African people
Must come together as
one tribe

Catch the vibe
Catch the feeling
Because it's amozeke-receiving!

IF:

Your family is a tribe
Going back,
Going way back,
To when Nzingha was alive….

Catch the vibe,
Catch the feeling,
If you amozeke-arrive!

THEN:

The gift of being is amozeke-receiving!
There is a reason for fate,
IF you keep amozeke-believing!

YOU JUST GOTTA AMOZEKE BELIEVE IT!
YOU JUST GOTTA AMOZEKE RECEIVE IT!

IF:

Your family is a tribe
Going back...Way back,
To when Shaka was alive...

THEN :

The gift of being
Is amozeke-receiving!
There is a reason for fate

IF,

You keep Amozeke-Believing!

You just have to Amozeke believe it!
You just have to Amozeke receive it!
You just have to Shaka believe it!!
In order to Shaka receive it!!

YOU!

Of the African race-
Keep on amozeke-arriving
Knowing that you are
Amozeke-surviving!

KEEP UP THE PACE!

Take it high,
Take it low!

RUN WHERE EVER
THOSE FEET CAN GO!

Take it high,
Take it low!

BECAUSE IT'S AMOZEKE-RECEIVING

WHERE EVER YOU GO!

Amozeke! Amazon! Amozula!

Amozeke! Amazon! Amozula!
when no one else can...
It's the mother of all mothers of
a foreign land!

When I was sick, they nursed me...
when I got well, they rehearsed me...
when all hope seemed lost...
here's the legend of your

Amozeke! Amazon! Amozula!
in the place of no winter frost!

Amozeke! Amazon! Amozula!
Quite legendary!

Amozeke! Amazon! Amozula!
Quite Extraordinary!

Amozeke! Amazon! Amozula!
So the whole world can see...

Amozeke! Amazon! Amozula!
How much you Amo-mean to me!

Amozeke! Amazon! Amozula!
From river to river...

Amozeke! Amazon! Amozula!
No different from one, or the other!

The A in Amozeke... wider than the river!
The M in Amazon...for the love the
motherland has given her!

The O in Amozeke...to keep us
going strong!

The Z in Amazon...because you'll
never forget this song!

The U in Amozula...wider than the river!

The L in the Love
She has given us:

And the U in Amozula!

Amozeke! Amazon! Amozula!
Restore the place-

Amozeke! Amazon! Amozula!

Back to our ancestors place!

Amozeke! Amazon! Amozula!

Restore our riches...

Amozeke! Amazon! Amozula!

Put the thieves in ditches!

Amozeke! Amazon! Amozula!

Make the crooked places straight!

Amozeke! Amazon! Amozula!

Give the dry places rain for the flowers to mate!

Amozeke! Amazon! Amozula!

Land of Kings and Queens!

Amozeke! Amazon! Amozula!

Will never see an end to their reign!

Amozeke! Amazon! Amozula!

Because seeing is believing...

Amozeke! Amazon! Amozula!

That your hope in them is Amozeke-receiving!

Amozeke! Amazon! Amozula!

Will always make a way...

Amozeke! Amazon! Amozula!

So that no one takes away!

Amozeke! Amazon! Amozula!

A peoples so strong and proud...

Amozeke! Amazon! Amozula!

A rich heritage so sing it out loud!

Amozeke! Amazon! Amozula!

I'm so proud to announce...

Amozeke! Amazon! Amuzula!

Is such an invincible force!

Amozeke! Amazon! Amozula!

Take from thieves hands...

Amozeke! Amazon! Amozula!

And restore it back to the mother land!

Like the Z in Amozula!

Back the motherland!

Will Amozeke-receive you from evils hand!

Amo-sing it out loud and wear it proud!

From one place on earth to the other...

Amozeke! Amazon! Amozula!

LIKE NO AMO-OTHER!!!

Amozeke! Amazon! Amozula!

I love Amo-yula!

I Amo-am,

   What I Amo-am,

   Like no other Amo-Rula!

Amozeke! Amazon! Amozula!

   When no one else can...

   Is the mother of all mothers of a foreign land...

When I was sick, they nursed me...

When I got well, they rehearsed me...

Amozeke! Amazon! Amozula!

When all hope seemed lost...

Amozeke! Amazon! Amozula!

In the land of no winter frost!

Amozeke! Amazon! Amozula!

No ordinary...

Amozeke! Amazon! Amozula!

Quite extra-ordinary!

Amozeke! Amazon! Amozula!

So the whole world can see!

Amozeke! Amazon! Amozula!

How much you Amo-mean to me!

Amozeke! Amazon! Amozula!

From river to river!

Amozeke! Amazon! Amozula!

For the love the motherland has given her!

Amozeke! Amazon! Amozula!

Wider than the purest ocean!

Amozeke! Amazon! Amozula!

Is more than just a notion!

Amozeke! Amazon! Amozula!

Makes waves over the ocean!

Amozeke! Amazon! Amozula!

Is more than just a notion!

Amozeke! Amazon! Amozula!

So the whole world can see!

Amozeke! Amazon! Amozula!

How much you Amo-mean to me!

The A in Amozeke, Wider than the river!

The M in Amazon…for the love the motherland has given her!

> The O in Amozula
> To keep us going strong…

> The Z in Amozeke
> Because you'll never forget this song!

> The U in Amozula
> Wider than the river…

> The L for the love the motherland has given her!
> To keep us going strong…
> The A in Amozula…
> Because you'll never
> Forget this song!!

Amozeke! Amazon! AmoAfricans!
searched high and low all over the lands!

Like the A in Afri-can
Like the M in Muzonta
Like the O in Osei
Like the Z in Zutundra
Like the E in Effect
Like the K in Korac
Like the E in Effect
And the K in Korac

Mountain so high!
Valley so low!

Mountain so high!
To the river it flows!

Mountain so high!
Valley so low!

Mountain so high!
To the river it flows!

Like the A in Amozeke!
Like the M in Moshesh!
Like the A in Amozeke!
Like the Z in Mozique!
Like the O in Zutundra!
Like the N in Otunba!

Like the O in Zutundra…
And the N in Otunba!

Live on in Amazon, and reign
eternal-zon!

Live on in Amazon, and reign
eternal-zon!

Live on in Amazon....
and reign eternal-zon!

Live on in Amazon...
and reign eternal-zon!

Like no Amo-Other!

Because seeing is believing!

Like no Amo-Other!
Because the thrill of conquest
Is amozeke-receiving!

Lawnmower Noise

Growing and growing
and going gallore...
Growing and growing
So give me some more...
Come back, boogie-woogie blues...
And show me what you got
In store...

All the right moves,
All the right grooves,

Is what you got in store...
All the right moves?

All the right grooves,
And all the right moves,
Hearing that lawnmower noise...
Waking you up
from a snooze!

Lawnmower noise as he
passes her by...
Lawnmower noise
He plans on the sly!

All the right moves,
All the right grooves...

Taking you up,
Waking you up,
Shaking you up blues!

Fade to black
Back to screen...
Save the drama for
Your mama
And you know what
I mean...

Save the drama for
Your mama...
Writing prose that's
Really mean...
Somebody's got to do it-
And that's me!

Give you,
Serve you,
Some boogie-woogie blues!
While hearing that
Lawnmower noise...
Puts you out of
the mood!

Lawnmower noise,
Lawnmower noise,

Hearing that
Lawnmower noise...
Waking you up
From a snooze!

Because temptation
and curves are
steadying his nerves,
So give the mistro
Some nitro, just like
friends and lovers should!

Put a band-aid on a blister,
Because them boogie-woogie blues
Can't miss ya'!

Genuine Moses...
No one knows this...was the affair...
Saint turned into skeezer,
So that men can go
To pieces...
While picking themselves up
The people, places and things,
And only the righteous!

Scratch and sniff first...
Dreaming again
So that hangovers
won't hurt!

Growing and growing
And going gallore...
Growing and growing
Louder than lawnmower noise
them boogie-woogie blues
are knocking down
opportunities and doors...

So strive
Arrive!
So I can
Give you some more!

Two

We're two...
Soldiering
Birds of a
Feather and
Yes, we all
Stick together
Like two peas
In a pod...
I know I've got
A hot bod-

Who's to say?
Who's to deny?

These things won't
free you if
They're all lies...

That's my name
so don't wear it out!
The uncle- tomstress'
Likes to sing and shout
Nothing but insults...
If the shoe fits
She's gonna wear it....
Miss 'em diss 'em...
And also his clout!

While making you feel
So brand new...

Wanna hear my
Broken record?
That's news you can use...
Wanna hear my
broken record?
Hears news to relay!

Because two...
Soldiering
Birds of a feather
Like a team...
They always stick together....
Like two peas
In a pod
I know I've
Got a hot bod-
That's my name
So don't wear
It out-

Have to be careful
Have to have a plan!

So that we don't fear
the bounds!
Or be teetering on the edge!

fatal attraction sits on
a ledge
Waiting... for cupid to
nod yes... to send it
On it's way-

To us...as two lovers
tread ...
into the sunset...
to live forever
Until two lovers are dead!

Saint Turned Skeezer

Saint turned skeezer
Pretend or do you
Believe her?
Who would have known…
It's a lie outgrown!

Saint turned skeezer
Nothing but a teaser
Who would have known
Unless you didn't keep
your own

In check--
No man had a hard time
getting respect…
Unless you didn't keep
your own
in check--
There wasn't no man
who was a saint
wouldn't believe her!
She just saint…
And at night
She's a skeezer!

Would turn men on
Would turn men off
With lavish spending
And fast cars at night
By day a round of golf!

She says it's just a notion
I've got a mind deeper
than the ocean!
And that's a natural fact
She said devil get back
Wanting to do what's right...
Misfortune is always at arms
length
And prosperity out of mind
Out of sight

I've got a mind that's deeper
straight hair is when
you receiver!

Saint turned skeezer...
Pretend or do you
Believe her?
Who would have known   ...It's a lie out grown!

Way up North!

Poor little Lizzy-Lizzy
wrote them a note- saying
this is how you make it on
freedoms boat

Way up north!
Way up north!

saying this is how you
make it on freedoms boat

Way up north!
Way up north!

I'll never-ever blame you if
the beast don't float!

Because if it does
and if pigs fly...

I'll stick a needle
in the masters eye

On freedoms boat
If the beast don't float

All hands up high
Till they reach the sky

Forever won't pass
and freedom last
like freedoms boat
on freedoms hope

Forever won't pass
and freedom last
On freedoms hope
If the beast don't float

Way up north!
Way up north!

Hands up high
Till they reach they sky!

Way up north!
Way up north!

I'll never-ever blame you
If the beast don't float!

Hands so free
And hands so high!
-Stick a long needle in the
masters eye

Went right in-
What it take to stop the sin!

Way up north!
Way up north!
If the hope was gone
    then the life was born
And the promise was sworn
On loves lost lorn

But freedoms boat-
in the life that float-
Then forever won't pass
And hope will last!

Poor little Lizzy-Lizzy
wrote them a note
saying this Is how you
make it on freedom's boat-

Way up north!
Way up north!

because on freedoms boat
in the hope which last
to the long -gore- long
just to sing you this song

Way up north!
Way up north!

On freedoms boat
If the beast don't float

Because if it does
and if pigs fly
I'll stick a needle in
the masters eye!

Way up north!
Way up north!
Way up north!
Way up north!

Rowing Machine

Stowing,
Knowing,
Showing,
Growing,
Rowing machine!
Like two peas
In a pod,
And you think it's
mean!
Furious, word to
the mother!
Your own prodigal
brother!
A wiff of fresh air...
It's not bitter
Or bare,
Differences of opinion
Brains: God gave you some!
So use them!

Stowing, knowing,
Growing, showing,
Rowing machine!
Is twice the competition
And you think it's a dream!

Over oceans and streams,
though impossible as
It may seem...

Real is our love
Love is our real
As white as a dove
Like a hand in a glove
We fit together...
Through all kinds
Of weather!
Two of a kind...
Gonna make you mine
Two loaves...
Five fish...
Yes two loaves,
And yes! It was a miracle
In love all is fair!

Racing ahead
Never being misled,
Miracle worker!
Like no amo-other!

It's smooth as silk,
And never to bilk,
folks out of millions...
Because I'm a person...
Ten to one zillion...
I'm a person-not one
One the world, but living
Amongst millions

Don't you want to go there
Streets of gold...

Diamonds and pearls
We all love to wear…
Seek higher learning
As high as eagles soaring!
Seek higher learning
And you will be growing!
He connected water

To dry land
Heaven is above
the earth,
as we all
Understand!
Gonna shake it!!
Because I'm gonna make it!
He's got a master plan!
You gotta leave it in His hands!
He's got a master plan
And a master mic-
While thunder rolls and
lightening strikes!
That parted the red seas!

Stowing, going,
Knowing, showing,
Rowing machine!
Like to peas in a pod
and you think it's mean!

Real

If it's not real
We must conceal
If it's not in the brain
We must contain!

No pain
No gain
No pain
We must contain

No shots
No loss
No shots
Come count
The costs

To change-
Our hopes rearrange
The costs-
In you the Amozula
In the land of no
Winter frost!

If it's not real
We must conceal
If it's not in the brain
We must contain!

No pain
No gain
No pain
We must contain

No shots
No loss
No shots
Come count the costs

Live Love

Live, love
Laugh out loud...
While heads are up
walking tall and
speaking proud!

Live loud
Die proud
Give until it hurts...

Live loud
Die proud
Show loves worth...

worth seeing
worth believing!

All things become
brand new
One heart made two
He leads me into directions
No inhibitions
Or imperfections

Live, love,
Love live!
Live loud
Die proud!

Give-
Til it hurts
While the waves roar
loudly and while
the surfers take off
their shirts!

Live, love,
Love-live...
Hold on to the beauty
That you got to give!

Way up north
Or way down south...
Give all you can
Or just shut
your mouth...
Open it to reason
If you think
This is tough
Just call it treason!

Love live
Give what you got
Because you got giving
When the going gets rough!

Hungry Thieves II

And now that I've made my grand escape,
All the grub that is, could have been was,
But as sure as skies are blue,
I've shared with them food and also motherly love!

There is a place I have
Which is my favorite pub
It's hidden not in my house
It's a place of brotherly love

If there's something I never ever want to see
It's thieving and robbery
They eyeballing everything I have...
Seems like the thing they need is brotherly love!

I'm starting to think that it wasn't enough to give
They want me to keep leading them...
As much as like I'd be breeding them,
Long lost family they are not,
They're not too old to be a have- not!

I'm starting to think that motherly love wasn't enough
Watch who you freely give to...
Because you'll never know what you'll get in return...
At times it's a matter of being smart-and tough!

Listen up you hungry wolves
And listen up good!
I works hard and saves...
Just like you all should!

Five days a week
Sometimes without rest
Somebody had to have bought ya'll into this world
Because they are not lost friends from my nest!

Towers of food!
Shelves of wealth...
But this time they won't find none!
I ain't do this for my health!

For if they came running after me...
Following me to my secret place of wealth...
They'll just wonder who it's for...
This I'll just have to keep for my self!

Because hard times are ahead...
And maybe they don't have the slightest notion...
That I know they came here from somewhere...
To plan a takeover and set it in motion...

To fight fire with fire I must do...
And this be my utmost observation
To come to conclude that what I call logic...
Will cause them to wander all over the nation!

Don't come for my grub!
My house ain't no pub!
Don't come back no more!
I don't live in a store!

Place to place
Searching face after face
From to and fro
And going back and forth

What a sight for sore eyes...
Those wandering fools will be...
Forced to roam and wander around...
Instead of following here and there after me!

Because ever since I fed them my apples
They seem to step two more feet...
But how did they find my storehouse
Because their doom they just might meet!

And what else has done this?
But them apples I fed them all ...
They are truly on a mission...
I wish I could shrink 'em two sizes small...

My fool heart had to show them sympathy...
Was the biggest mistake I'd ever made...
But now it has to be back to the drawing board...
while I sit under the tree, sipping lemonade...

It's time to fight fire with fire!
Because these fools are in the wrong place!
There's got to be some way I can make 'em go...
Run them out of my town- It'll be a race...

I got more tricks for treating...
Some rude old rogues like that...
They can stick their ugly tongues out all they want...
Don't care- I didn't lay 'em out no welcome mat!

Because there's one thing I know...
And this I say for sure...
My home is where my heart is...
Because for thievery like that, there's
a solution and cure!

Eternal hunger pains do some damage...
A tornado leaves lives in despair...
Wondering if I have to be a miracle worker...
Until their attitude is no longer: "We don't care!"

Seems as if what's mine is becoming theirs...
Seems like all of a sudden!
But they came from who knows where...
Somebody got long lost friends because I doesn't!

Whatever happened to the good ole days
When you lost something you cared to find it...
When parents kept their kids on a tight leash
And when nobody would ever even dare to mind it...

Whatever happened to the good ole days?
When you fought temptation and won hands down?
When kids were their parents pride and joy...
And they made sure that duty kept them around...

But now seems like all that has changed...
Maybe changed for the very worst...
The good old days are gone forever...
Now you outlive your kids because they dies first!

But as sure as I live...
I know things have to change this day...
Because If folks want to eat...
They must learn to work and obey...

I work hard all day
And labor hard for what I got...
But how did these folks seem to escape...
Like prisoners breaking out!

But like prisoners busting out
Is how they going back in...
Like dogs back to their masters
By their collars to be reeled back again...

To learn the value of hard work...
Back to what they consider to be a prison...
They must learn to obey and follow rules...
Dollars for doing nothing is what they won't be given!

But as sure as I live...
I know things have to change this day...
Because if folks want to eat..
They must learn to work and obey...

May seem like sunny days are gone
When all you see is rain...
It seems that hungry thieves feel so low...
Needing some kind of escape to ease the pain...

But joy cometh in the morning,
And tomorrow another day...
We all have our share of suffering....
Because one day, our tears will be wiped away!

Horse

If I had a horse
It would say a whole lot...
If I had a thirst
That would hit the spot

Take a ride
Or wade in the ravine!
Venture on the Nile
Or jump through a stream!

I can't speak on it'....
Walking in new shoes....
Just go on and take them!
And hold on until it gives
You the blues!

IT'S GONNA MAKE YOU SURE!
THAT YOU WON'T HOLD BACK!
AND THEN YOU ARE DOWN...
MAYBE ENDING UP IN A SHACK!

This is what I'm saying to you:
What I'm relaying to you is true...
That's a natural fact...
NO I wouldn't lie to you
You took that!
Now see how hard it is...

TO WALK IN MY SHOES?

Now see how easy it is...

When I start to giving

YOU THEM BLUES!?

BUT WHEN YOUR TROUBLE COMES...

JUST KNOW WHERE IT WILL TAKE YOU!!!!

Feet Brand New

I like the way
the crowd roars
when he comes
dashing through
the doors!

Drive yourself!
Revive yourself!
Life is a chore...
Sweet blessed Jesus

Open up some doors!

Feet brand new
Hands brand new...
Why wait?

Feet brand new
Hands brand new-

I'm safe!

Dreamboat

It's you!
Poetry is you!
Light the sky up
Because the stars are blue
And my days are sunny

No life without flowers...
Climbing tall towers...

Clothing the young ones
From head to toe
Making sure they fed
Never let 'em be misled

If you never getting
Nothing in return...
If the bun's not taken
Out the oven- it burn!

Dreamboat, steamboat,
Don't shake ya' head

Dreamboat,steamboat,
All the mouths must be fed!

Somehow, some way,
You had some fun
For a roll in the hay...
For a little
Heaven on earth drug...
For a sweep under the rug...

Patience once a virtue
But no longer today...
The guilt will mount
Hope will wither away

Like dead flowers
Dreamy, fine...and
Tall like towers!

Are you for real?
Or are you fake?
All it takes is once
Then it all be a mistake

Are you for real
Or are you fake?

Baptize, realize,
That heaven won't wait!

For a dreamboat, steamboat,
to get straight!

Wisdom

The wisdom to see,
The knowledge to know...

That old motherland,
That old motherland...

See her grass gardens,
And watch how they grow...

That old motherland,
That old motherland...

Beat the drums fast,
Beat the drums slow...

That old motherland
That old motherland...

Dance to the rhythm,
Move on with the show...

That old motherland,
That old motherland...

Watching my gardens,
And watching me grow...

That old motherland...
That old motherland...

Ugly Cats

I turned around and what did I see?

It was a bunch of ugly cats

Was just looking at me!

It was a bunch of ugly cats

Was just looking at me!

I turned around
and what did I see?

One eye-No eye...
No hair-don't care!

Three legs, peg-legged...

Their alienation...

Grumpy and bumpy

and fed up with starvation!

For not one year, but two!

They been sitting there so long

That they ain't know what to do…

But now it has come to this…

I have to get to the store,

And it's me against an army of cats

Somebody has shipped them to my shore!

They were born to stretch

And multiply from one to one million!

So just keep on feeding them

Have to start and keep breeding them!

But now it has come to this…

Have to let the story end or go on…

It's ten times Rembrandt!

And then they were gone!

But now it has come to this…

Have to let the story

End or go on…

It's ten times Rembrandt!

And then they were gone!

Trail Blazers

If ever you wonder
How I be...
Expressive, wonderful, giving...
That's me!

I live life
Love-live...
I love the beauty that she gives...

I love the rain
I love the snow
Just giving you the best
Just knowing what's in store...

If ever you wonder
How I be...
Expressive, wonderful, giving...
That's me...

I live life
Love-live...
I love the beauty
That she gives...

I love the rain
I love the snow...
I love what she gives
And then some mo'...

Give me some more seasons
And I'll give you so more reasons...

Take my hand
To the promised land...

Take my hopes...
And give me something dope...

Take my hand
To the promised land...

Make me free...
Make me believe!

The Baroness Lizzy

The Baroness Lizzy,

Lizzy to the bore,

The Baroness Lizzy,

Don't speak no more,

You go south to east,

And east to west,

You spend each day,

Knowing what is best!

The Baroness Lizzy,

Lizzy to the bore,

Folks downtown don't

Want you to take it no more!

She sees what she sees,

It is what it is…

But the mobsters got her

All wrapped up in they bizz'...

Baroness Lizzy,

    Lizzy to the bore...

    Ruling the underworld

    Till they speak no more...

    Baroness Lizzy,

    Lizzy to the bore...

    Ruling, and schooling

    Till they hear it

No more!

Baroness Lizzy-

The Baroness Lizzy Lore!

Her house-her castle...

Tongues wagging

They pants sagging...

Baroness Lizzy,

Lizzy to the bore!

Speak to their conscience

Till they hear it no more!

Baroness Lizzy,

Lizzy to the bore...

See it - believe it

Dream it- scheme it

No more!

Strutting My Stuff

I plunge forward and take a dive in the pool of life
I find food, clothing and shelter
From gray clouds of a fools frivolousness
Loom ground to sky
And all around...
One to choose and one to make a choice...
Just see what's in store for you...
I've got a smile turned upside-down
And the suns so big
It's gonna wash away all my cloudy days...
Turn rainy days into sunny ones...
Got a smile so big I put it on the sun ...
So the sun's got a smile and eyes like mine
I'm gonna turn around, turn grapes into wine...
Fill all the clouds with rainbows
So that your empty head can be filled with dreams...
Fill all the earth with beauty and precious things...
So your head can empty out its schemes...
Every bit of happiness is heaven to me...
I'll cheer for you and you'll cheer for me...
I'd rather love him than leave him
He makes me feel lovey-dovey, girly-wurly, see...
Because the more I learn to outsmart them fools...
The more them backstabbers will burn
With jealousy, with rage, with hatred for to learn...

Save what you want and save the best for last...
Because my life is not a stage
And you show ain't gonna watch
So just get the hell on off your but!

So are you gonna get off your butt and leave?
Why don't you just strut-
To the next town, city or state...
By plane, train or automobile,
Before you find yourself in concrete shoes...
And yourself in a big rut...
And when the door is open
I'll have a song in my heart
When the door is shut
I'll be so happy
Wouldn't know where to start!
I'll get up and strut...
I'm gonna strut my stuff!
I'll keep a song in my heart
I know just where to start...
Because this is a gem of an opportunity
I'm gonna strut my stuff...
And if you don't like it
Then so what...
Just mind your own business, see...
I'm gonna keep strutting my stuff!

The Dream

Sam had a laid back mansion,
And had a limo long, black, and sleek,
And had a garage to fit all of them,
Larger than next week!
Oh, how sweet life is for these
Rich folk,
Never wanting for nothing,
So I walk over to Sam
To pay him a compliment or something...
He invited me to dinner,
An evening drive
Were our plans for the day,
But he turned around to look at me
With such an evil face,
I had to get away!
I ran fast and swift,
Resentment I did harbor,
But the house went from grandoise,
To haunted funeral parlor!
The limo turned to hearse!
Didn't know which was worst!
Feeling so much fear and dread,
For in a moment I'd be dead...
I knew I couldn't turn to fight,
For I felt so much fright,
The fear I felt
I could not tell...

The mansion turned to house
in hell!
But pretty soon I learned my lesson well,

Be careful what you wish for...

Some dreams are a hard, cold, sell!

Samoseam

Samoseam! is the beautiful dream,

...and the beautiful

dream of you!

It's the beautiful view-

And the beautiful dew-

And the things I do for you!

It's the beautiful scheme-

And the beautiful dream-

And the beautiful wonders

of what life can be-

Samoseam! is the beautiful

dream...and the beautiful

dream of you!

It's the beautiful view-

And the beautiful dew-

And the things I do for you!

It's the beautiful scheme-

And the beautiful dream-

And the beautiful wonders of

what life can be!

Samoseam- the beautiful dream...

Samoseam- the beautiful scheme...

The Creed

Once, twice is an amazon...

Once, twice to play this song!

Once, twice, singing one,two, three!

Once, twice, because I aim to please...

Once twice is an amazon!

Once, twice just singing my song!

Once, twice, and you were once there.....

Once, twice, and I did not care...

Once, twice, what folks thought of me...

Once, twice, and all there is to see...

Once, twice, all there is to being me!

Once, twice, it was just you and me...

Once, twice, we both aimed to please!

Once, twice, from shore to sea!

Once, twice, is an amazon...

Once, twice just singing my song...

Once twice singing one, two, three...

Once, twice, and all to being me!

Once, twice is an amazon...

Once, twice, just singing my song!

Once, twice, and you were once there...

Once, twice, and I did not care...

What others thought of me...

Once, twice, because this is the creed!

Pipe Dreams

Pipe dreams,
Pipe dreams,

More of a piper-sniper!

Pipe dreams,
Pipe dreams,

Something of a

Pleasure delighter!

Schemes, not dreams,
Are having their way,

Because have-not
Ain't got
For years of dismay!

Pipe dreams,
Pipe dreams,

Bet on a dummy…

Pipe dreams,
Pipe dreams,

Lose all your money!

Sit there and wait...
As you build up more hate...

You wear a weave...
Because you wanna receive...

Pipe dreams,
Pipe dreams,

Forget to remember...

Pipe dreams,
Pipe dreams,

Speedy December!

Pipe dreams,
Pipe dreams,

Are having their way...

Pipe dreams,
Pipe dreams,

Are having their say!

Pipe dreams,
Pipe dreams,

See it and believe it...

Pipe dreams,
Pipe dreams,

Straight hair is when
You receive it!

Pipe dreams,
Pipe dreams,

More of a piper-sniper!

Pipe dreams,
Pipe dreams,

Something of a
Pleasure delighter!

Schemes, not dreams
Are having their way...

Because have-nots
Ain't got-
For years of dismay!

Be there
Be Square
Be Low
Be Whole

Be There
Be Square
Be Low
Be Whole

Person

I'm just a person
One in one million!

I'm just a person
Ten to one-zillion!

Here I stand
Though I'm not tall

The more you build up...
The higher the great fall!

I'm just a person
Ten to one-zillion!

I'm just a person
One in one million!

Here I stand
Though I'm not tall...

There's nothing in the world
I won't do for you at all!

I'm just a person
One in one million

I'm just a person
Ten to ten-zillion!

Here I stand
Though I'm not tall

There's nothing in the world
I won't do for you at all!

The Word

The word is pleasing
to the senses
and sounds tempting
to the ears

Like drugs can get
you high to believing

And make you feel
so damn good receiving!

Until-It makes your whole head spin!

Makes me feel
so damn low-
why you walking so slow-

Makes me feel
so damn low-
drama is like a show!

Makes me feel
so damn low-
why you walking so slow-

Makes me feel
so damn low-
drama is like a show!

      The word is pleasing
to the senses
and sounds tempting
to the ears

Like drugs can
get you high
to believing,

And makes you feel
feel so damn
good receiving...

Until it makes
your whole
head spin!

Makes me feel
so damn-low!
Why you
walking so
slow?

Makes me feel
so damn-low...
drama is like
a show...

Makes
me feel
so damn-low

Why you
walking
so slow?

Makes me
feel so
damn-low...
drama is like a show!

One Ace

I got big trouble, big love
from the heavens above

is where cupid come from
then he drum-beat-drum!

His arrow shot me...
then he up and got me!

Two hearts one ace
Then a smile on his face...

He laughed at me shuck
it all...once it was elusive...

it was far, far, far...

Now hear it come nearing
at the doors...

I don't want to know
despair no more!

These waves can't
hold no weave!

As we remember the
things we're about to
receive!

Drum beat drum....
say you sway...
And he up and got
Two hearts one ace!

Drum beat drum
say you sway...

And he up and got...
Two hearts... One Ace!

Man Hands

Man Hands...NO Indian giver...

Man Hands...Who'll ever out live her?

Your uncloudy nights
Turn dark skies from gray...

Your uncloudy nights...
Dance all your troubles away!

Man Hands...No Indian giver...
Man Hands...From hand to hand,
From river to river...

Man Hands...For the people
Hath given her...

Man Hands...One to cross the sea...
Another to cross the river!

Man Hands...Something you dare
Not say...

Man hands...Something you can
Relay...

Was one to rule ten million-
Something to make your day!

Man Hands! Always knew what
To do!

Man Hands! Like the moon, casts
A shadow over you!

Man Hands! You looked and saw
her standing there!

Man Hands! Will take you out
Of evils snare!

The troubled sea!
The troubled past!
The troubled sea...
To the rescue at last!

To bring you in headstrong!
To sing you a brand new song!

Man Hands! Forget your troubles
And past!

Man Hands! She's here at last!

Man Hands! NO Indian giver!
Man Hands! Who'll ever out live her...

Your uncloudy nights
Turn dark skies from gray!

Your uncloudy nights
Dance all your troubles away!

It was Man Hands...
The Indian hero!
It was Man Hands...
Won war after war!

Man Hands! The Indian
Warrior...

Man Hands! Who stands
Beside her...?

Man Hands...You'll never
Find another...

Man Hands...That was closer
To you than your own brother!

The troubled sea!
The troubled past!
The troubled sea
To the rescue at last!

The troubled sea!
The troubled past!
The troubled sea...
To the rescue at last!

Man Hands! Not your average
Leader...

Man Hands! Lived far away
And long ago!

Man Hands! Who is the greatest
Mystical ruler that you'll ever
remember and know?

Man Hands! Folks haven't
Heard enough...

Man Hands! Put the T in tough!

Man Hands! No Indian giver!

Man Hands! Who'll ever out live her?

Your uncloudy nights
Turn dark skies from gray...
Your uncloudy nights
Dance all your troubles
Away!

Man Hands! NO Indian giver!
Man Hands! Who'll ever out live her?

Your uncloudy nights
Turn dark skies from gray...
Your uncloudy nights

EASE ALL YOUR TROUBLES AWAY!!!

Make You Wish That You Was

The music to the beat
The rhythm is your drug
The music to the beat
Make you wish that you was-

To the music
To the rhythm
To the rhythm
To the beat

To the rhythm
To the music
To the music
To the beat

Make you wish that you was
An unhappy maiden
Married to a spinster
Make you wish that you was
Take two and two together
And mix them-

To the music
To the rhythm
To the rhythm
To the beat

To the rhythm
To the music
To the music
To the beat

I love the music
The music just in me
I love the music
To the rhythm to the beat

Make you wish that you was
The rhythm is your drug
Make you wish that you was
The rhythm is your drug-

To the music
To the rhythm
To the rhythm
To the beat

To the rhythm
To the music
To the music
To the beat

The music to the beat
The rhythm is your drug
The music to the beat
Make you wish that you was-

Old Man River

Sitting, wondering all their nights...

Being carefree all their days...

Freedom was the

Fight of all fights-

The right of all rights...

I'm gonna go tell it,

Go to the mountain...

For old man river

Took their tears

Wiped it off their faces...

God will as God will it!

Their freedom they

Was given it!

This was the story

That they told

They sat there thinking

Old man river

Had them sold

This was the story-

Of old man river-

This was the story-

Of the freedom

They been given-

And it seemed to take

Up all their time

Their freedom was given

For all times!

But what came next

Was the quiet storm

After the old man river

Freedom was the norm

They stamped out the devil

That made them perplexed

They stamped out the devil

Put them in hell with the rest

But don't put out the fire!

Made themselves comfortable

While taking themselves higher

With song-

The strong-

The young-

The old!

With song-

The strong-

The young-

The old!

Because old man river

Tried and true-

Took them to freedom

Under skies so blue!

The Tree

The tree

Is unstressed

The tree

Is a test

A test of brains
A test of wits

For no soldier
Ever quits!

The tree is unstressed,

A test of brains,
A test of wits,

See what He has
In store for you,

For no soldier
Ever ever quits!

The tree
Is unstressed,

The tree
Is a test,

A test of brains,
A test of wits,
For no soldier
Never, ever quits!

The tree

Is undressed,

Stands mighty
And blessed,

Stands the best
For a perfect mind,

Stands the tree
And the sands
Of time for all Times!

Mt. Kilimanjaro

But quietly I had
To slip away...
Not even less
Than a day...

So sound
Yet so gentle...
The winds may blow...
Almost swept me off-
Mt. Kilimanjaro!

So sad is
The inevitable goodbye...
See how grass grows
On my Mt. Kilimanjaro!

Lizzy's Boredom II

Lizzy's Boredom-

Boredom- to- the- Lizzy!

Betcha- bottom-dollar,

Gonna love it in the city!

Yes, Boredom Lizzy

Is her name

Swinging and swaying

And singing is her game!

If you look and see her

She's far away...

But if you look again

She just might be there to stay!

Lizzy's Boredom

Boredom to the Lizzy!

His eye is on the sparrow

Flying high over the city!

BE THERE
BE SQUARE
BE HIGH
BE LOW

BE THERE
BE SQUARE
BE HIGH
BE LOW

Listen!

Listen!

To the sounds
Of the drummer man...

And his discovery of
an ancient land...

Yet
in his hands lie fate!

Better hear how they
slow down fast
At
his masters command:

Mon Khessan: Average Man!

Where the trouble begins-
Lusaka Ends!

Listen!

To the sounds of the
drummer man...

and his discovery of
an ancient land...

but in his hands
lie fate!

Better hear how
they slow down fast!
At his masters command:

Mon Khessan: Average Man!

Where the trouble begins!
Lusaka Ends!

Mon Khessan: Average Man!
Where the trouble
begins...

Lusaka ends!

Kinks

I got kinks in my

ankle-

like kinks

in your hair....

I got kinks like

your mama in

Gucci underwear!

I live for

them pops,

I live for

them kinks...

I live for the rhythm

just the way that

you think...

I live for the band...

I live for the plan...

I live for them kinks

For just the way

that you think!

If it's in the rhythm

then you can

get with them...

If it's in the

air then I

don't care!

Kinks in my hair

thinks I don't care...

Kinks not long-john

Gucci underwear!

Red light on stop

and green to go...

Red light on stop

just to Gucci you

some more!

Red light on stop

and green to go...

Red light on stop

just to Gucci you

some more!

Kinks making links

like they don't care...

Kinks making links

on Gucci underwear!

I live for them pops...

I live for them kinks...

I live for the rhythm

Just the way

that you think!

I got kinks in my ankle

like kinks in your hair!

I got kinks like your

mama in Gucci underwear!

The Deed

See it!

Believe it!

Feel the dream...

See it!

believe it!

Instead of your schemes...

Try to make it plain,

Try to understand...

Feel no schemes...

Just live your dreams!

Feel no schemes,

Just living your dreams!

Breathe the air

Boogie-down

Gotta care!

And breathe the air

Boogie-down,

Gotta Care!

Let Us Be

You are you
And I am me...
A father meets the
Needs of one...two...and three...

Never forget
Always remember...
April-May romance,
Speedy December...

You are you,
And I am me,
Because God
Ain't through
With us yet,
So let us be!

Cats make
Your house smell...
And dogs wish
You well...

Never forget-
Always remember...
April-May romance,
Speedy December

You are you,
And I am me,
Because God ain't
Through with us yet,
So let us be!

Afrane Luminous

One great big beautiful land,

Once great, regal, and still grand!

Sits high to the motherland

Great and low!

The wisdom to see...

The knowledge to know...

Sits high to the motherland

Great and low...

The wisdom to know!

As great as a king can stand

Great land of the mother

Be free and grand!

Like NO! Amo-Other!

As great as any land can be...

Seek higher learning

From coast to sea!

Amozeke! Amazon! Amo–Africans!

Amozeke! Amazon! Amo-Africans!
Who ruled all over
The African lands

In Africa...
Where the trouble begins

In Africa...
Lusaka ends!

Where the Ugah-Jugahs lived
And the Ugah-Jugahs loved
Yes the Ugah-Jugahs
Lived under the
Heavens above

Where all the people
had ruled-
and they all was kin!

It's often hard to accept
where the tides
do begin!

So listen...
To the sounds of
The drummer man...
And his discovery
Of an ancient land...
Yet
In his hands
Lie fate!

Better hear how
they slow down fast!

At his masters command...

Mon Khessan!

Average man!

Where the trouble begins!

Lusaka ends!
Mon Khessan!
Average man!

Where the trouble
Begins...
Lusaka ends!

Amozeke! Amazon! Amo-Africans!

Searched high and low
All over the lands!

Like-

The A in Amo-Africans...
The M in Motunda...
The O in Oseikhu...
The Z in Zutundra...
The E in Effect...
The K in Korac
The E in Effect...

It makes you feel okay!

Mountain so high...
Valley so low...
Mountain so high...
To the river it flow...

Mountain so high...
Valley so low...
Mountain so high...
To the river it flow!

Amozeke! Amazon! Amo-Africans!

Reign-reign,
Reign-reign, all over
The lands!

Like-

The A in Amaze...
The M in Amazon...
The A in Amaze...
The M in Amazon...

The Z in Zulunda...
The O in Otumba...
The Z in Zulunda...
The O in Otumba...

AM-AM
ZO-ZO

How low can you go?!

AM-AM
Correct!

How high can you stretch?!

Amozeke! Amazon! Amo-Africans!
They ruled all over
The African lands!

Where the Ugah-Jugahs lived!
And the Ugah-Jugahs loved!
And the Ugah-Jugahs
Lived under the
Heavens above!

And listened
To the sounds
of the drummer man...

And his discovery...
recovery an ancient
Land...Yet in his
hands lie fate! In
his hands, why wait!

Better hear how
They slow down fast
At his master's command...
His masters command!
Mon Khessan!

Average Man!

Where the trouble
Begins !

LUSAKA ENDS!

Amozeke, Amazon
Of the African fate...

Amazon Mon Khessan
Of the average debate!

Amozeke, Amazon
Of the African fate!

Amazon ,Mon Khessan
Of the average debate!

Hand-in-hand...
From river to river!

From sea to sea
And hand-in-hand!
From sea to sea
I'm gonna say it again!

From sea to sea
And hand-in-hand
From sea to sea
I'm gonna say it again!

Amo,
Amo,
Africans!

Amo,
Amo-Africans!

the never-ending
rule all over the lands!

the never ending rule
while it's so grand!

MON KHESSAN: AVERAGE MAN!
WHERE THE TROUBLE
BEGINS...
LUSKA ENDS!

MON KHESSAN: AVERAGE MAN!
WHERE THE TROUBLE
BEGINS...LUSAKA ENDS!!!

Ain't Misbehaving

My hearts broken

Is what I'm believing!

Ain't misbehaving

Like you receiving!

Down right dirty

And and able-believing!

Ain't misbehaving

Like you receiving!

There ain't no vitamin C

In that cup!

So stop acting like

There is...

Vitamin C ain't

Going out...

And ain't none

Coming in...

Deprivation is a sin...

You just can't

W - I - N...Win!

Seeing is believing...

That you ain't gonna be receiving...

Vitamin C ain't going out

And you can't put none in...

You just can't

W - I -N , win!

    Why oh, why...

    You just was the

    Best!

    Why, oh, why...

    Is what I confess...

    Dig a ditch,

Don't feel dismay,

Dig a ditch,

Just have it your way!

I say what you gonna do,

When it falls down on you?

I say, what you gonna

do, when those walls fall

Down on you?

Wait out the storm?

Or sit out your troubles

Like a princess in a

High tower!?

Africa

Where traders trade,
Where musicians play,
Where dances sway hips,
Where villagers move lips...

Where princes dwell,
Where kings rule by the bell,
Blue are her rivers,
Yet deep are her thoughts,
Many are her injustices,
The pearls of wisdom that costs...

The price of knowledge,
The price of beauty,
The price of shelter,
The stolen diamonds and rubies...

The Power

Flower Power!
Because they wanna take them all away...

Black Power!
Because we're here to stay...

Love Power!
Kiss and tell!

Woman Power!
Rule by the bell...

Knowledge is Power!
Your brain is like a sponge...

Man Power!
Do it and get it right!

Universal Power!
Power to those who believe it...

The Power!
'Straight hair is when you receive it!'

Universal Power!
Power to those who believe it...

The Power!
'Straight hair is when you receive it!'

Black Power
Of the hour...
Straight hair- you gotta
believe it!
Straight hair is when
you receive it...

Black Power
Of the hour...

Straight hair-you gotta
believe it...
Straight hair is when
you receive it...

Black Power
OF THE HOUR...
STRAIGHT HAIR-YOU GOTTA
BELIEVE IT...STRAIGHT HAIR IS WHEN
YOU RECEIVE IT!

Dream, Dream, Freedom's Bell

The higher you build
The higher your fall...

The stronger the will...
The more power for us all...

Dream, Dream, freedoms bell...
Dream, Dream, eat to live well...

Dream, Dream, Wait your
Change...

Dream, Dream
May even seem strange...

Behold!
Dream, Dream...

As difficult as it may seem...

Behold!
Dream, Dream...

From anywhere in between!

Dream, Dream
Freedom's bell...

Dream, Dream
Eat to live well!

Dream

You know all I ever do
Is dream about you...
At night and at day...
In every given way...
The knights are at flight
With every sleepless night
Expressions flare!
Assume I care!

It's being specific
That keeps it terrific
It's the style of your hair...
It's the clothes that you wear...

You know all I ever do
Is dream about you...
At night and at day
In every given way...
The nights are in flight
With every sleepless night...
Expressions flare!
Assume I care!

It's being specific
That makes it terrific
It's the music you make
It's the rhythm you create
It's the clothes that you wear
It's the style of your hair

You move me
You groove me
You show me
You know me

Expressions flare!
Things you share!
How you dance for me...
How you chance for me...
How you walk with me...
How you talk with me...

Keep living
Keep giving
Keep being
Keep seeing

Keep dancing
Keep romancing
Keep seeing
Keep believing

Earl

Earl the pearl
The wisdom you took!
Earl the pearl
Write me a book!
Earl the pearl
So I can see!
Earl the pearl
Mean so much to me!
Earl the pearl
Like a bright sunny day!
Earl the pearl
Why don't you come my way!
Earl the pearl
If ever or never!
Earl the pearl
Through all sorts of weather!
Earl the pearl
Turn dark skies blue!
Earl the pearl
The many ways I show I love you!
Earl the pearl
You rock my world!
EARL THE PEARL-
THE PERIL!
THE WORD!!

Facing The Honest Truth Like Ruth

Getting to forget
Forgetting to get

To have and not to hold
To hold and not to fold

Giving to receive
Forgetting to believe

Anxious to make a bet
And so willing to receive

Facing the honest truth
Standing here with Ruth

Having somewhere to go
And going with the flow

Knowing you, knowing me,
Showing you where to go,
Showing you what I believe,

Just believe it...
So willing to receive it...

Nothing's farther than the truth...
I'm facing it just like Ruth...

Nothing's farther than the truth...
I'm facing it just like Ruth...

Long Gone

You once was lost but
Now you're found...
Betcha bottom-dollar
Spent on the town...

You once were here
And now you're there...
Telling me a tale that's
Totally square!

Oh, sing us a song!
String us along...
Sing after we're long gone
And make merryment
On and On...

Long gone,
Long gone,
So far away...

Long gone,
Long gone,
Though you were
Here to stay!

Could it be the beginning
Of a brand new day?

Could it be the end
Of an old family way?

Fair-crossing you
From left to right...

Swinging and swaying
To a song such a wonderous
delight!

Could it be so wrong...
We are in the great race...

Could it be so wrong...
Scandal could be such
A total disgrace!

Long gone,
Long gone,

How led astray...

Long gone,
Long gone,

Refusing the family way...

For the love of money
And all for status...

For the love of the honey
And everything that matters!

Long gone,
Long gone,

What's a person to do?

Long gone,
Long gone,

Just when you thought that
You knew...

Long gone,
Long gone,

Knew enough to know
about the family way...

Long gone,
Long gone,

Knew enough to show
Your faith and stay...

Long gone,
Long gone,

Right by my side all the way!

Long gone,
Long gone,

So far away...

Long gone,
Long gone,

That you might be
here to stay!

I Must Lead

Though I can be led
I must lead...
Because they will follow
I must succeed...
Gonna drive
And be driven...
No I won't waver
At the outer limits
Of the moons crater...
Though I can follow
I must lead...
They will not stay
But only stray...
I have no care
I have no worry...
Because a leader
Leads a tribe...
And tribes need a leader...

Lord lead me to a
Brighter day...
Because the good Lord giveth...
And He taketh away...

Though I can follow
I must lead...
North to Northwest..
West to Northeast...
Others can hope
What they cannot see...
No I won't lead
Those too scared
To follow...
The rest can have hope
And for a better tomorrow...

Have-Not Less-Got

Stupid is
As stupid does...

Pretty is
Just what it was...

The more I give
The more you take...

When your
Trouble comes...

Just know for sure
What it makes...

Have-not
Less-got

Have-not
Less-got...

...To be such a showoff!

Stupid is
As stupid does...

Pretty is...
Just what it was...

The more I give
The more you take...

When your trouble
Comes...

Just know for sure
What it makes...

Hope

Hope is the
One lone
Cry
In the wind...

That the devil
tempted Eve
to sin...

Peace be still
And peace
To you
Again...

Hope is the
One lone
Cry
In the wind...

Hungry Thieves III

So now, what's this? You say...
It's a hungry thieves part three!
Well tell me, say it ain't so...
It just wasn't really meant to be!

So I'll put it this way...
And here's what I said:
At long, long last
Those hungry thieves are fed!

At long ole last
Twas a breath of fresh air!
Like a page from a story book...
In love and war, all's fair!

The memories rung a bell
And it gave you some laughs...
A story that serves you well
And gives you joy at long ole last!

Those hungry thieves I fed
They went from sup- to super!
It felt really really good
Once I turned them into my troopers!

There's no place like grub
When your house is a pub!
There's no place like grub
Make your house a pub!

I Live In A World

I live in a world...

And the world
goes around...

Where the hunted
And the hunter
Wears the pants
And something big is
Going down...

I live in a world...

And the world
goes round..

Change...

And give me change...

Come as you are...

Just stay the same...

For a Little Heaven on Earth Drug

I was born
I was raised

here on earth,

I was born
I was raised

'Came right from the dirt...

Oh yes, indeed
it's me in the need,

Found a quarter
in the dirt...

Blow it off don't hurt!

I'm here to stay-
I cry-I die!

Have to kill some bugs...

In a valley so high!

I squashed them devils
In the dirt...

found a quarter on the ground
but what was it worth?

Dog gone-gone dog
Play fair-Be square!

For a little heaven on earth drug-
For a little sweep under the rug-

For a little heaven on earth drug
In the bottomless pit up above!

Dog gone-gone dog
Make them devils disappear

Dog gone-gone dog
Show them no fear!

For a little heaven-on-earth-drug!
For the beauty up above

Show them no fear...
Fear them no show...

In the valley up above
For A little heaven on earth love...

I'm here to stay...
I cry, I die,

Had to crush the opposition
In a valley so high!

Valley so high
Valley so low...

Valley so high
To the river they flow...

Valley so high
Valley so low...

For a little heaven on earth drug...
For a little sweep under the rug...

For a little heaven on earth drug...
In the bottomless pit of love!

Bright Eyes

Bright eyes
As bright eyes blue
Warm embrace
And tender are you
When you're next to me
Are thoughts so real
Thoughts of loving you
And things which
Always do appeal…

I want you near to me
As you are dear to me
Take my hand
Let's go to the promised land
Take my hand
Not hard to understand…
So what's the big deal?
Is you rolling like a wheel?
And the heart of you's for real
And the heart of mine you steal…

Ashy

Ashy lips! need
constant zip!

Crabby old wooden legs

Crabby old wooden and she begs
For attention she wants
But wasn't getting none...

Trouble wouldn't come
Till she searched for some...

Fat, old clumsy hands,
Flying through sea, air, bodies, and land...

Button your cracked lips
And take your hands
Off your hips...

I want you to change
Quit trying to rearrange!

Your foolish ways
Will be the cause of your downfall!

A Girl Called Stupid

A girl called Stupid,
is her name...
A girl called Stupid,
playing her game...

A girl called Stupid,
is her name...
A girl called Stupid,
Playing her game...

Once was lost,
But now she's found!
There's no more pretending-
She's heaven bound!
A girl called Stupid
Served her time well...
A girl called Stupid
Sometimes you can never tell...
If Judas wasn't a traitor
This I know for sure...
She used her time well...
   But will love be the cure?

A girl called Stupid
With the glasses on her face...
A girl called Stupid
Is now a fighter for the human race!

A girl called Stupid
To change for a season of change
A girl called Stupid
Her time has come to rearrange!

A girl called Stupid
Stand once and for all
A girl called Stupid
Was no name to be called!

Stupid was bad
As we understood...
Stupid now fights for the common good!

A girl called Stupid
Is her name
A girl called Stupid
Playing her game
Once was lost
But now she's found
There's no more pretending
She's heaven bound!

The Talk

Love hurts because Eve sinned...
Poverty exists because Adam gave in...
And took a bite from the apple
of the tree of knowledge of
good and evil!

So Adam took a bite,
He thought he was right,
Gods patience was worn thin...

So instead of coming out-
He going back in...

The closet is a walk-in...
Keep your baggage in there
And do what's right!

Wider Than The River

Amozeke! Amazon! Amozula!

Is not just a notion!

Amozeke! Amazon! Amozula!

Far and wide
all across the oceans!

The "A" in Amozeke
Wider than the river...

The "M" in Amazon
For the love the Motherland
has given her!

The "O" in Amozula
To keep us going strong...

The "Z" in Amozeke
Because you'll never forget this song!

The "U" in Amozula
Wider that the river...

The "E" in Amozeke
For the love the motherland had given her!

The "Z" in Amazon
To keep us going strong...

The "Z" in Amazon
IN YOU THE AMOZULA!!!!

Dreams And Desires

My dreams are
Fading away
Fast!
I hardly
Have time...
Because dreams
Are like
Rare gems
And rare finds...
Once one
Has designs...

My true
Loves lorn
Lost...
Rare and
Fading away...
Count the
Cost...

What do I do?
Where do I go?
Seeds that you plant...
Seeds that you sow...

But what do I do?
Where do I go?
Seeds that you plant...
Seeds that you sow...

The Escapade

The escapade is all about
love, devotion, and honor...
And never betray what you follow!
Always forget and never remembering...
our hearts are made as one,
The oddities...
The drama has our hearts as one,
They hollowing us love inside,
When the evil creeps around
Why should we hide?
We should fight!
To try to put those things
Out of our sight!

Our sight,
So that they creep around...
The oddities,
Trying not to make a sound...

So before they turn back
And try to destroy the cause,
Put it in reverse
Or you better pause!

Nothing's gonna stop us now,
The drama!
Your mama!
May pop us loud...
Right side, upside the head
To keep common sense
Trapped in...
Locked in the brain instead...
If you can count,
You are prepared,
For the rain
So let it be never misled!

The escapade is about,
Love, devotion and honor
And never betray what you follow!
That's why we fight
The evil that creeps around quietly
And so-called, innocently,
Turns around to war against us
To fight
The drama,
Your mama,
The us!
Your mama is who you trust!
With all your life
so let it show
them whose boss!
Paying the price and
We paid the cost!

The oddities were following
Us all around...
For they seek to destroy...
After being kind, clever,
and coy!
And for that reason,
They seek to annoy...
So they need to get lost!
Coming out of their dead...
And still being misled,
It's the heart and the mind
that has died the death as well!
So the zombies seek,
So the zombies hide
Like a pack of soldiers
Waiting to jump out of hiding,
To come outside!
The pain
The joy,
The drama,
The ploy!
The us...The joy, in who you trust!
Seeking to destroy,
Persistence is a must
Insistence by those
who will only sit by and rust!
While they decide
Whether to fight or hide!
We're the pure!
We're the sure!
We're the hard-workers...
We have the cure!
And that's why...WE WILL DESTROY THEM!!

For Real

Yours being lost in the cracks of society
Yours being tossed in the wind
Like a windmill-
Can't you see?
You were everything a brother
Should be-for real...
You were everything...
Once poor and pressed,
Now here's the deal...
Stressed or arrest,
The competition wore a vest...
Stressed or arrest,
There are witnesses who have
Seen the very, very, best!
The very best of them,
While your life is flashing by...
Isn't that what it's all about?
To give it the old college try
But if you'd rather die than cry...
Wait for real...
And change, then get changed...
And that's the deal-
No lie!
Rearrange the plan...

So your heart can feel
It beat again...
Better believe it!
Straight hair-don't care...
To better receive it!
Be for real,
My heart you steal,
Always at your best,
Whether poor, or pressed...
Be for real,
For real to be,
-Not always suffering...
Because you're always tougher
And that's the deal!
Yours being lost in the
Cracks of society...
Yours being tossed in the
Wind, like a windmill...
Can't you see?

Hate

Hate: the illusion!
Rust: Until your brain is
a contusion!
This is what it makes you:
Hate until it breaks you!
Don't do it...
Or try to think
You can go through it...
Never let them see you sweat...
Become an achiever,
and you'll never have
any regrets!
Achieve!
So you can go forward!
Believe!
In the things people
get more of...
This is what it makes you...
Hate until it breaks you!
Got a mind to get through it...
So move!
It's not a suggestion!
Prove!
Is not the only question
That folks are going to have
For you...

Amozeke-believing
In all the hate....
Amozeke-receiving
All that is great!
Beauty but a curse...
Brains, but a reverse
In misfortune!
Giving you heck...
And putting you in a wreck!
Go through some pains,
Walk through the rain,
And while you're at it
Hope you feel forced
To do nothing but complain,
Go through it
Get on to it
Even though sometimes
It may not be much fun
Then folks will see
The inner beauty in me
The outward conspiracy
Which they try to reach
Hate is what it makes you
Hate until it breaks you!
Not last, not least,
Sad, ugly, sick or deceased!
I ain't dead,
I'm gonna get ahead,
Whose nickels and dimes
Are lost...
Dig them up and count the cost
Of the sacrifices
And the prices
That were paid for you!
Now is the time

To gather up and be strong
Not sit around and be blue!
Hate: the illusion!
Rust: Until your brain
Is a contusion!
This is what it makes you
Hate until it breaks you!
Do or don't
You will or you won't
Try to get on through it...
So be not a follower
Got to lead!
These things must free
your mind if you want to succeed!
Are You Ready?!

Spread Love

But if you want American music
I say
Pat Boone...
Spread the love
Spread the joy
Because God gonna come soon!
Sooner is better than later...
Or is it that you're a couch-potato?
Here I am
At last!
Here I am!
Soon, death will be a part of the past, so...
Take your phone off the hook...
And rest up with your favorite book.
Straight hair is when you're receiving peace...
The violence against us should just cease!

Better whenever you delay it...
Ideas that you can relate to
And never quit!
So it's better late than never, I say...
Free your mind before you under the dirt!
Got to always pray!
Prayer is the essence of survival
A perfect new life in the world
WAS HIS ARRIVAL!

Spread the love!
Spread the joy!
with tradition...
and Zeke-Ambition...
While building up nations
and closing life's doors!

And when you find the sun is
still shining rays and showers...
You will be amozeke-arriving
On trains and tall towers!
That gives the race cars speed,
while at that supplying all
your needs!
Yes the train was blue
Not a sad one,
but fast enough to make
you say: Glory- Hallelu!

How can you feel
It's just pretend?
That there aren't a lot of
Ways to tell a true friend...
So relax after a hard days work,
And folks won't go thinking
In their minds you're a jerk!
So who is the first?
The first and the last...
Erase all your worries
And let it be a thing of the past!

Spread love
Spread the joy
So that you can hear the story

Of the miracle baby boy!
You know the name,
You know the legend,
You know it's more
Than ancient history
And more than the luck
Of number seven!

Remember the first
Remember the last
Remember the traces
In your past!
SPREAD LOVE!
SPREAD THE JOY!
...With tradition...
...And Zeke-Ambition...
...While building up nations...
...And closing life's doors!

SPREAD LOVE!
SPREAD THE JOY!
...With tradition...
...And Zeke-Ambition...
...While building up nations...
And closing life's doors!

Perfect World

Why can't this be a
Perfect world??

Let this old one crumble
And come to an end!

Why can't this be a more
Perfect world…

Where despair and misery
Is not my constant
Companion and friend

It's the good one that got away!

So what's the use in trying
To stay in between a rock
And a hard place?

-Kept the faith while
Running this rat race

-Kept the faith while
Feeling this dark and
Dismal disgrace,

Separate but equal
In separate beds,

Separate but equal
Wishing for a paradise land!

A more perfect world
In a better place-

A more perfect world
Will end a rat race!

That had been going on
Since times past,

That had been going on…
So I could be freed
At last!

Time flies when you're
Having fun,

If I'm a worldly woman
I'm not the only one!

May have been stuck
In this rut or here to stay,

It still might all be pretend…
More than sunshine
On an uncloudy day!

But in this perfect world
I will find my place

Which will be where ever
I want…
So get out of my space!

Perfect world,
Perfect friend,

Perfect world,
Is it only pretend?

A more perfect world,
In a better place!

A more perfect world
Ended a rat race!!

Greatness Found

Greatness found
Greatness lost
Amozeking everything
You thought was boss!

Arriving at the solution
Is like being king!
Not cursed, but blessed
In everything!

Put it to the test
While never really
Laying it to rest

Put it on pause
And fight hard
For the cause!

When you have
The upper hand…
And fight hard
For the cause

Like you was
In the motherland!

I fight with a big
Stick…
Because my mama
Raised me like this!

Greatness found
Greatness lost!

And when you feel
So good
You're singing in the
Cold rain…

Just count the cost!

Greatness found,
Greatness lost,

Amozeking
Everything you thought
Was boss!

Arriving at the solution
Is like being king!
In answer to your question,
It recreates in you
The amozula in everything!

And making you turn
Every which way
But loose…

Greatness is only
Found in God's
Golden truth!

So when greatness
Is found
And greatness lost,

Just face the honest
Truth…
And you shall be boss!

You will arrive at
The solution
Which is like being king…

Not cursed,
But blessed in everything!

The Blood

How do I know?
Because the blood told me so!
I said ask me how I know
Because the blood done told me so!
Just like Cain killed Abel
When he died
The blood didn't tell God no fable!
So he couldn't hide!
Nothing's far from the
Honest truth...
I'm standing here
Facing it like Ruth!
The blood can tell a lot,
Because a Lie will
Stay on a liars mouth.
The blood will tell
Because a liar is just
Going to fail you
Through in and throughout…
And let you down quick-
Don't forget Cain, and Abel...
Don't forget the stick!
If you only can see
The ugly truth and how it's
meant to be...
All a bad dream
And a thing of the past

All a bad dream...
But are we really free at last?
Be pure and true...
Let the music all blast ...
-you away-
As real as we can be...
I sent the cats out to play....
It's me, I'm free...
It's real, so why don't
You just let it be!
It's me, I'm free,
It's real...So why don't
You just let it be!

Perfect Fit

Indirect, distant interpretations

Better tight-knit families,

Tribes and nations!

I've got the answers

I've got the key-

Faith is the weapon

Fear get to steppin', see...

Driving the answers

Out of your brain

So that we won't

Go insane!

Strength is what will

Drive you-it's the key-

I've got the answers

To all of your misery!

And let it be a perfect fit…

Like a new shoe

So be it…

Let it be a perfect fit-

Hope is the one lone cry-

We all need it!

Open Road

If a lie is the truth
And the truth is a lie…
I'd just as sure as fail
When I succeed
And be succeeding
When I fail to die-

For a worthless cause

I say youth is inner beauty
And someone says as much
As that Rudy…pause!
Because things are gonna
Be like that…
I'm still writing the
Kind of prose that rocks--
I'll be on the attack!

For a little heaven-on-earth drug
For a little sweep under the rug

For a little heaven on earth drug…

In the bottomless pit of love!

Rat Race

This rat race,

This gangster pace,

Has always been

Where it's at,

Because they

Can't fight…

Can't get it right…

In this rat race dwelling

On the past!

They got back where,

They're supposed to be

Where, nobody can see

At last!

I'm tired-

Ain't going nowhere…

Better believe it…

I've got straight hair…

This rat race is always

Where you receive it!

Always stressed

But never impressed

I ain't dying or dead

Because the music

Because the rhythm

Had left things unsaid…

So go ahead

Complain to Fred

Why can't they get it right?

At last a breath of fresh air,

A blast from the past

Makes you go from slow

To full steam ahead!

So you can run this rat race,

Keep going the gangster pace,

And always know where it's at!

I can't complain,

To keep from going insane,

And always know where

It's at!

Gonna move mountains this time,

Gonna bust a stupid old rhyme,

Gonna make you feel the rhythm

For the truth we are always going

To be given…

Got to keep running this rat race

Got to keep up this gangster pace

Because that's always

Where it's going to be-

This old rat race!

Piglatin

Piglatin…

I'm making things happen,

Things are going to slow down,

Don't plan on stopping me now…

Don't go away mad,

Don't hang around-

Leave or be glad…

For the heaven-bound

For that virgin sound

Piglatin!

I'm making things happen,

Experiences for rapping,

So instead of coming out-

He's going back in

Just to be attacking!

And if you don't like it

You cease to know the deal…

Get to stepping out of my door

But be for real!

Educated

Success is hell,

And poverty is heaven,

Six is the beast,

And yours the lucky

Number seven!

Because thugs and bugs

What you don't want to see...

Thugs and bugs

Only bring you misery!

Thugs, bugs and drugs

In your neighborhood...

Thugs, bugs and drugs

Ain't never going to

Be nothing that's good!

Everyone stressed,

Until we all become blessed…

Come together,

All birds of a feather,

So you can see…

That your history

Ain't no mystery

So

Get educated!

The Winning Hand

A thing of beauty
In life won't last

A thing of beauty…
Put the "T" in task…

If your life's a sensation,
Then I'll make headlines
And waves all over this nation!

Which dance floors are solid ground,
So that indecisiveness is virgin sound,
Make headlines for the cause today..
Get educated- go all the way!

Which do you choose
Which do you lose,

You've got to play your
Card hand right…
For whatever your fate is
Got to make a little educated guess

Live, love, learn…

Pass the test! Gain insight!

For it's the winning hand!

The Virgins

Truth is a dare,
Take it or leave it…
Knowing God's legendary history,
Is when you choose to receive it!
Now the virgins had sticks
And the virgins had stones…
The virgins got them running scared,
So folks swore they'd leave them alone,

They went in with their sticks
To beat the devils down
Because devils got their kicks
Bringing them down!

And as they vowed to cheat old death,
The virgins got guns…
Because they wasn't working
For their health!

So they went into their own garden,
To see if the roses behaved,
Because the virgins are a mighty number…
Christian folk who never go astray!

So now that you know
The virgins, their numbers and the show…
Will always have folks running scared

So just leave them alone-

Riper-Viper Pastures

Either the experiences
Are bitter…
Or they are sweet…
Riper-Viper pastures
Is such a bubbly, tasty, treat!

And it got you in a wreck
It's gonna give you heck,
It wasn't yours,
It was mine
Because we are two hearts
Made one
Two hearts got their lives!

These things must free your mind
If you wanna play- Are you ready?

For riper-viper pastures
Are you ready?

We're going home
We'll gonna fly away
And our pace is always steady!

Been Born

I've truly been born
I've truly been sworn
To protect and serve

I'm torn
Been born
Why you wearing my pearls?

What are the words
Because I had forgotten them
To have you to hold you..
To wash, dry and to fold you…

Truly been born
I've been sworn
To silence and secrecy
And to heighten this legacy

I'm torn
Been born…
Juggling some dreams

I'm torn
Been born…
Cooking up some schemes

Juggling, smuggling, and struggling
To keep goals alive
Juggling, struggling, and struggling
To amozeke-arrive!

Higher Plane

Bright-brained, educated and trained…
Bright eyes as bright eyes blue tamed…
He's revolutionized the world
And the worlds got to revolve
Into a hope brand new!
He's revolutionized the world
Into a place that's so brand new!

If you close your mouth
You wont have to holler
Stream, river stream,
Because the river runs opposite…
Chasing you
Embracing you
That's running wild
Was the excited child…

Bright brained,
Educated and trained,
Higher plane…
Jesus and God are One
And the same!

-Place He once was and is as before…
In that place called Eden
One day the angel blocked the doors…
Choose, don't lose
So that we can be winning-receiving…
Creation, the power and the glory
Means a whole lot more!

Because the end
Justifies the means
Will be different
Until busting out at the seams
Just waiting to receive you
Because this world is a stage…
Just wanting to believe in you
On a higher higher plane!

-Where there's room for both of us…
Brighten up the skies too much
-Where there's room for both of us
And the pipes are clean
Copper will always rust!

Choose, don't lose,
The power is us…
Choose, don't lose-
Your faith-or you'll only start to rust!

Your Mind

Your mind is a dangerous weapon
So if folks don't like how I relay it
Then folks can get to steppin'!

It's the hope where creation
Is all brand new…
It's the help where the word is bond
And the coward's eyes gets
Turned black and blue!

Shield and spear
Will protect you in your
Secret endeavor…
And that your hope in
Amozeke, Amazon Amozula

Is the new weapon!

Your Mind That Place!
Good God The Race!
Your Mind That Place!
Good God The Race!

Some say the imagination
Is a dangerous weapon
And as creation is made
The imagination is a dangerous weapon!
Peep this, keep this,

Or just get to steppin'!

Your Mind, That Place…
Good God, That Race!

Your Mind, That Place…
Good God That Race!

Your Mind, That Place…
Good God, The Race!

Your Mind, That Place…
Good God That Race!

The Young

The youth need only to realize
The young must truly recognize

We need to amozeke-strive,
So that we all can amozeke-arrive1

Us together, like birds of a feather
Let us all keep hope alive

The youth need only realize…
The young must truly recognize-

New hope
New dreams
One and the same
But so far and few in between!

The youth need only realize
The young must truly recognize

Eternal youth
Everyone wants it…

The eternal song
You're gonna want to sing
Dance and flaunt it!

For a little heaven and earth drug
For a little sweep under the run

In the bottomless pit of love!

The youth need only realize,
The young must truly recognize!

Snakes and the Legend

Snakes and the legend
Yours, the lucky number seven…
Safer if you go north
Disgraced if you move south
Prosperous if you are east…
Honored, if you move west!

That is why number one is wise
These things must free your mind
If you wanna play…Are you ready?

Loyalty is what drives you
With straight heads
It's seeking to arrive with you…

Because some people
They don't understand
If we know our hearts..
Then we're always home,
In the motherland!

Snakes and the legend
Yours, the lucky number seven

Coming and going,
Learning while we are turning,
Every which way, but loose…

Yours the lucky number seven,
Snakes and the legend!

The Lovers

The lovers of the world are hopeless
It's tearing me apart going coatless!

But more and more I see the change
Shipped to shore
Oh, how they rearrange!

The world needs to adjust
But more and more
I see the change
Or, God, we rust!

You're all that's fine,
Footloose and fancy free
And all that's original
Making eternal history!

You're all that is simply wonderful
That's why I'm feeling, being free
You're all that's simply wonderful
That's why I feel no misery…

The lovers of the world are hopeless
It's tearing me apart going coatless!
But more and more I see the change
You're all that's fine, footloose and
Fancy free-

Try to rearrange!

Wanted

Seeking a different
Kind of artist
With a different kind
Of vision

Seeking a different
Kind of world with
A bolder kind of wisdom-

Who was it
Who does it
On the right road
All the way home!

Who was it
Who does it
On the right road
All the way home!

Walking to the beat
Of a different drum
Seeking someone who
Walks hand-in-hand

With sticks for a drum!

To the beat,
To the rhythm
Of a drum-beat-drum

To the beat
To the rhythm
Of a son-of-a-gun!

Seeking a different
Kind of Artist
With a different kind of vision

Seeking a different kind
Of world with a bolder kind
Of wisdom!

Better Days

Better days are coming soon
If you don't like what I'm saying
Then look at the moon!

Better run this race
Must take first place
Because you'll never finish the run
If you don't wake up-
Then you'll miss the morning sun!

Let's free our minds
Because we wanna play,
Soon is soon
For a bigger, and brighter day!

Hands off the drag queen
Hands out of the cookie jar
Or you'll make the drama mean-
So much more in pictures
Than words can express
So much more in pictures
Than words help to pass the test

Believe
Better days are coming like rain

Receive
Because bad dreams can
Drive a person insane!

Keep running that race
-Must take first place
Better days are coming soon
As the world goes round the sun
When you walk into the room!

Relate!
Don't hesitate!
Arrive!
We must survive!

Don't stress
But try and pass the test,
And there won't be no repulsions…

Believe
Always receive
Instead of going into
Convulsions!

Better days are coming fast
If you don't believe what I'm saying
Then get out of the past…

Wake up out of your sleep,
And just turn over a new leaf,
Blaze a trail and forge a path…
Blessings you receive
Always free at last!

Soon to come are better days
So go ahead and let the haters rage!
Be a winner
Not always a beginner
Strive fast!
Death will be a thing
Of the past…

Be a winner
Not always a beginner
Strive fast!
Death will be a thing
Of the past!

The Joy

Life's a hero sandwhich
With a brassy, sassy song…
Wa'tusi on Lucy
Singing it all night long!

All the joy Watissimo!
If you blink
You miss it more!

What is it except
Another bad creation
What is it except

Living, laughing and loving
In God's glorious elation!

All the joys of life's despair,
Innocent until proven guilty
Because a white lie is
Only a snare!

All the joy Watissimo!
If you blink
You miss it more!

A Finer Line

A much finer line
Between good and evil
A much happier time
With the people you
Believe in…

It's the quickest,
It's the hippest,
Amozeke-receiving…

It's the quickest,
It's the hippest,
All that is worth perceiving!

A finer line,
A happier time,
For the folks you
Believe in,
Who are always
Amozeke-believing!

A finer line,
At the fastest pace,
A finer line,
In order to finish this race!

More hope to come,
Soon your work is done,
Achieving more dreams
That you can reach,
A little heaven on earth drug,

And a finer line,
So let's keep trying,
-To teach!
About a new world renown
So that only the world we can see!

A Finer Line Part 2

Some say that the mind
Is a dangerous weapon…

So you can either peep this
Or get to steppin'!

A finer line is a better place
A finer mind good God
The race!

A finer line between
Love and hate,

A finer line because
Heaven won't wait

A finer line between
Good and evil

A finer line can only
Make you a believer!

Give It A Rest

What you get out of hard work
Is success…
Keep on striving
Keep on arriving
Or just give it a rest!

Because they are building
You up just to tear you down…
They are building you up,
So that they can always
Hang around…

Rome wasn't built in a day
If I say leave
Then you best not
Try to stay!

And when it was burnt down
They had to try and survive
To build a better town…

And that's why the
People won't give up
And the people
Won't give it a rest…

The people won't give up
Until they passed every test!

Success!
Just give it a rest,
Because they're
Building you up
Just to tear you down…

They're building you up
Just to set fire to your town!

And the people didn't
Give a damn…
And the people won't
Give it a rest…
Because you've got to
Try and survive

So try to pass this test!

Downhill

If there's a chance
It doesn't seem correct,
And maybe a chance
I might have been
Giving folks heck,
Then try to understand
By and by…
Try to never recommend
Living, giving, on the sly…
Because it's like driving
At breakneck speed…
When in a world so selfish,
And seeing nothing but greed,
Life seems hellish-

What's a world without relics
Of a nation reborn…
Of your brightest shining hour
When your shame was shown…

Trust as you know
Is the story that is told
Betrayal is only for the weak
And truth for the bold…

The strong will survive,
As only the righteous can tell…
The strong will survive,
As they eat to live well!

That's the world we live in
Straight is the road
And narrow is the path
To a world renown!

Those were the days
When TV shows made sense
Those were the days
When it wasn't past tense…

Never learning
Never growing
The evil deeds men do
Headed to reaping what
They are always sowing…
Because one day our lives
Won't be so blue!

Downhill it's gone
And not original…
It's gone forever
And sure is pitiful!

Going downhill
Searching for a cheap thrill
Passing the buck
While the preachers today
Are down on their luck

On the heavenly train
On our way to a better world
On the heavenly train
Giving your dress a twirl!

You must learn to leave
Your cares behind,
And let your worries be few…
Take caution to the wind,
In a world so perfect and
So brand new!

The Rarest Folk

The rarest folk
For a different stroke
As we walk to the
Beat of a different
Drum-beat-drum…
We haven't got long,
A brassy-sassy song,
Even if you're out of tune
Or drunk and high strung!

Life you're given…
Hard knock life you're living…
Sweet Georgia Brown
And the world loves
A winner now!

Sassy song
Say it all night long…
The smell of time,
By the bell and the rhyme!

The rarest folk
For a different stroke
And a little heaven-on-earth drug
For a little sweep under the rug…
To the beat of a different
Drum-beat-drum!
In the bottomless pit of love
He gonna see it gets done!

Get you some knowledge
For the rarest folk
Get you some knowledge
It takes a different stroke!

For the rarest folk
And the drama queen…
For the rarest folk!

Because the drama is
Still mean!

The Answer

I arrived at the question
So what's the answer?
Where all the nations
Are unsure…
And all sins still like a cancer

When all else fails
Let love prevail and be
Like the only cure…

When all else fails
You have to always be sure…

At the start of a whole
New beginning
As we reap what is sown
Out of good…
Only then are we winning
With a brand new start
In the neighborhood!

If you arrive at the question
You'll get the answer
You'll have it all for yourself,
If only you take a chancer!

If you're not for-realing
In your life,
Then you are fake…
This world is in such disarray
That it distorts your vision
In a negative way…

So try to be stronger
You'll last a whole lot longer..
It's the only answer
So now just take a chancer!

The High and the Mighty

The high and the mighty
Got your back
The high and the might
Must always be on the attack!
For a little heaven-on-earth drug…
For a little sweep under the rug…
For a little heaven-on-earth drug
In the bottomless pit of love…

The high and the mighty
Rivers so deep…
The high and the might
Rivers do wide…
Face the honest truth
Face it just like Ruth…
Die together!
Wearing silks, satin or leather...
No matter going north
Steady headed south
If you're not singing in tune…
Then just shut your mouth!
Change while living east,
And be blessed in the west
Or delusions for illusions that
Are tricks of the mind
At their very best!

The Ends the Means

This race
This world
This gangster pace
Has always been
Where it's at
Right where it's supposed be…
In a world that never was flat…

Until…
The end comes surely,
Until…
The end comes silently,
Until…
The end comes swiftly,
Until…
The world ends defiantly…

The ends
The means
The Amozula
Who wins

Let love live!

The ends
The means
The Amozula
Who wins?

Let love live!

A flower
A choice
The rose
The song

Millions standing strong!
Millions singing all the
Day long!

Your hopes, dreams, and
The power…
Your hopes, dreams and
The trying hour!

The Good Song

It was the perfect ending
To a marvelous beginning
It was the baddest song
You've never heard
Anything so strong!

And makes love last
The whole night long…
Then you're only winning…
Let love and the living
Make earth spin on and onnn….

Can't get it out of my head
It's only good
Because you'll never be misled…

It's the good song
That keeps you rocking
All day long…It's the good song,
Makes you feel you can
Last all the night strong!

Until all hearts have bled
Love lasts and is strong…
Least and least said
It's the good song!

So use it,
Never abuse it,
Just love it,
And rise above it…

So use it,
Never abuse it,
Just love it all your
Life long…

Because that is the
Only perfection
From something so strong!

Meet and Greet

And if you're down for it

You'll love it!

Meet and greet

I'm a part of it

I'm above it!

Meet and greet

Makes life so sweet

And you've got the

Upper hand…

Folks will learn something

They all can understand!

Here I am

I'm here at last!

Here I am

Death is a part

Of the past!

Meet and greet something great

Meet and greet something

So grand....

Meet something so sweeter

Than the legends

Of the motherland!

Meet and greet

The One with the master plan…

Meet and greet

In the Amozula land!

Meet and greet

During this great endeavor…

Meet and greet the finer ones

No matter what the weather!

Meet and greet

The One with the

Master plan..

Meet and greet

In a world so grand!

It's Clear

It's only clear to me and them…

That your understanding

Is at the level of ten!

Falling apart and washed away…

Gotcha sold in your mind

While the waters rage!

It's clear you are seeing

Things that aren't there..

It's clear your are believing

That you lost your hair!

It's clear you can't read

The words on the page…

Hands off the drama queen

While she's on the stage

Visions of sugar plums

Putting you in a trance

Visions of sugar plums,

Making you wanna dance!

It's clear there is confusion

On your part

It's the only thing coming

Straight from your heart…

It's clear to me

That now your understanding

Is the level of number three…
So listen and read the only

Good book…

Listen and read

You're only a dumb crook…

Because trouble is the only

Thing you're gonna see…

You'll reap what you sow

Out of your own misery!

Start using your head…

Everything sacred and good

Won't be last

Won't be the least…

Or totally dead…

Somebody's Sweet Fool

The joy

The privilege

The loner

The liar…

And the sweet music
Has the base in your face
While lifting you up
A little bit higher!

Somebody's sweet fool…
Makes you wanna
Break them golden rules…

Got an angel on my shoulder
Give me the strength to
Walk proud and be
A lot more bolder…

Putting you in range
While taking you higher…
Making you feel something strange
So just put out the fire!

Somebody's sweet fool…
Needs to go back to school…
Quit trying to pretend
That a bad habit
Is your bestest friend!

Can you stand in the rain
While breaking them golden rules again…
Can you try to pass the test…
Until you find yourself
A total mess!

The joy
The privilege
The loner
The liar…

Because the music
Has the bass in your face
While lifting you up
A little bit higher!

www.ingramcontent.com/pod-product-compliance
Lightning Source LLC
LaVergne TN
LVHW021657060526
838200LV00050B/2391